"This book is readable, relatable, and doesn't rely on confusing or technical language. It's an important read for everyone, especially women, considering a career in the industry. Juli does a great job capturing ways in which you can truly help your clients, which is what this career is all about."

—Caroline Feeney, CLU,® ChFC®
President, Prudential Advisors, Prudential Financial

"Juli's book is a wonderful reminder that our profession can be customized for each person's strengths and vision. I was touched by her candor about her struggles and it reminded me of many of my own. Her message of survival, focus, self-talk and teams give all of us more tools to move through the rough more quickly and get to more of those 'bursting moments.'"

—Michelle Hoesly
Past President of MDRT

"This book proves that this isn't just a 'man's world.' The possibilities are endless for women in the insurance industry—they just have to know where to look. Juli's book is the first place."

—Brian Ashe, CLU
Past President of MDRT &
Current Treasurer of LifeHappens

"*Juli writes from the heart about the possibilities of success for women in the insurance industry. Creating and working your plan is the key, and Juli's book provides you the guidance to craft your personal blueprint.*"

—Marvin H. Feldman, CLU, ChFC, RFC
President and Chief Executive Officer, LifeHappens

"*If you're interested in learning how to achieve an attainable work-life balance, while also dedicating your life to serving others then this book will provide valuable insights to help you achieve that success.*"

—Jennifer A Borislow
President Borislow Insurance, 2012 MDRT President

No
NECKTIE
NEEDED

I wish you great success!

All My Best!

No NECKTIE NEEDED

A Woman's Guide to Success in Financial Services

JULI McNEELY

Securities and Advisory Services offered through SII Investments, Inc. Member FINRA, SIPC and a Registered Investment Advisor. McNeely Financial Services, Inc. and SII Investments are separate companies.

Certified Financial Planner Board of Standards Inc. owns the certification marks CFP®, CERTIFIED FINANCIAL PLANNER™ and federally registered CFP (with flame design) in the U.S., which it awards to individuals who successfully complete CFP Board's initial and ongoing certification requirements.

Printed in the United States of America

ISBN Paperback: 978-0-692-68182-4
ISBN eBook: 978-0-692-68183-1

Library of Congress Control Number: 2016905380

Table of Contents

Invitation to the Reader 1

Chapter 1 | You Deserve to Be Successful
Because You're Good, Not Because
You're a Woman 5

Chapter 2 | The Industry Is Set Up for Men,
Not for Women—And Why Financial
Services Is Actually a Great Field
for Women! 17

Chapter 3 | The Flexibility Factor: Financial
Services Lets You Balance Your Roles
Like No Other Career 27

Chapter 4 | Women Make Great Leaders, Too 37

Chapter 5 | Why Women Function Better With
a Team 49

Chapter 6 | Transitioning Your Practice: Why
Are There So Few Mother-Daughter
Teams in Financial Services? 59

Chapter 7 | Saying No to the Negative Voices
in Your Head 67

Chapter 8 | Avoiding Misunderstandings in
Business and Social Settings 83

Chapter 9 | Insurance Is No Longer a Hard Sell:
It's Taught and Bought 97

Chapter 10 | How Defining Moments Can Show
You How Far You've Come. 109

Chapter 11 | Redefining Success: It's Always
Your Choice 127

Invitation to the Reader

On SEPTEMBER 11, 2012, I STOOD NERVOUSLY behind the curtain at Caesars Palace in Las Vegas. I wasn't worried about a wardrobe malfunction, some complicated dance steps, or hitting all the right notes. From my seat in the audience, I'd just been texted that I'd won the election and was now the next secretary of NAIFA—the National Association of Insurance and Financial Advisors—40,000 members strong, more than a century old, and the most formidable trade organization in the industry.

I'm not sure I can describe the joy and anticipation bursting from every cell in my body at that moment. The feeling was beyond almost anything I'd ever experienced. As I stood backstage that day, as if that victory wasn't enough, I knew in just two years I would become the first female president in NAIFA's 125-year history. I absolutely knew it.

But how did I get there? Not a week has passed in my twenty-year financial services career when something remarkable hasn't happened that doesn't prompt me to ask myself that question! I mean it: How did all this happen?

I am an ordinary woman from a town of 1,925 people in central Wisconsin. There's nothing spectacular about me, my family lineage, or the schools I attended. I did my homework, had afterschool jobs, did chores at home, and played sports. I struggled with self-confidence and still do, and grappled with ideas about a career. I ended up feeling nameless and lifeless in corporate America before making a giant leap into financial services where, for all intents and purposes, I started all over again.

If you had asked me at the financial services three-year mark—fraught with so many challenges I was about to give up—if I'd have greater financial success than I could ever have imagined, I'd have said you were crazy. If you had asked me at that three-year mark if I'd be good enough at my job to help lift a looming financial burden from thousands of individuals and families, I'd have said you were crazy. If you'd asked me if I'd become the first female president of NAIFA—that I would be able to accomplish something on such a grand scale—again I'd have said you were crazy. But it happened, and it did so because I finally got out of my own way, worked hard, and focused on believing it would.

My life keeps me up at night—not so much because I dwell on my accomplishments but because I know it is possible for you to have your own string of victories in financial services. I want you to have what I have—and more. I know what's possible in this industry, and as a woman who's forged a long road to the top, I want to help you get there too.

Chapter 1

You Deserve to Be Successful Because You're Good, Not Because You're a Woman

As AN ASSOCIATE TV NEWS PRODUCER IN 1970, Mary Tyler Moore raised eyebrows and consciousness at a time when women were on the threshold of a revolution at work. Many times in the decades that followed, it appeared the scales tipped one way or another, with women relegated to the same old mold or else promoted to fill burgeoning quotas, just because they were women.

But success isn't gender-specific, and though financial services is still a male-dominated industry, today more than ever the industry is a place where women can determine their own value and self-worth because they are good at what they do—not because they are women.

While the industry presents its own unique set of challenges for women, there are qualities they seem to espouse more than men that groom them for the job, or tailor the industry to them, depending on how one views it. These include a propensity for ferreting out and recalling details (personal and otherwise), cultivating relationships, and investing time and energy in educating people. These will be explored in greater detail as we move through the book.

In this industry and others, **women don't always know just how good they are,** and if someone praises them for their accomplishments, they may not believe it, or own it as the saying goes. Consequently, they don't use it to promote themselves and advance their careers the way men typically do.

When I went to work in financial services in 1996, nearly three decades had passed since TV's "Mary Richards" had flung open some key doors in the workplace. Still, I knew I was going into the proverbial gentlemen's club—or men's room—maybe one of the last bastions of such as we entered the new millennium. The industry was set up by men, for men, and for the most part training was geared toward more direct, cold, hard "just the facts" kinds of sales that did not favor the way women are likely to approach a client. I knew I'd have to work very hard not only at mastering the material, but at breaking through barriers and establishing relationships in my own way to gain a foothold. If I couldn't do that, success would be out of reach.

In addition to the gender disparity, while achievement was surely my goal, the last thing on my mind was replicating a job I'd seen my hard-charging father do since the day I was born. I knew I didn't want to do things the same way, and if I eventually took over his company, there would have to be a transformation in the way we did business. Where the emphasis for him was on regimented selling, playing to my strengths as a woman I wanted to focus on educating and creating relationships with clients—and staff—more than forging a practice built on hammering out transactions. I figured that's how I would continue to grow my father's business and make it my own.

On the surface, the industry had seemed to steal my father from his family. Because he had spent so much time building his business, all I knew was his absence and I'd decided early on that kind of life just wasn't for me. I had to do things differently. I was striving for a work-life balance, and I believed the financial services industry could lend itself to that.

Interestingly, though, I didn't come willingly to the table—at least not at first.

After college and a degree in marketing, I ended up not finding the public relations or advertising job I coveted and went to work at a large national bank in Minneapolis. At the four-year mark, I knew corporate America wasn't my cup of tea. I worked exceedingly long, hard hours and watched the vice presidents earn their annual $4 million bonuses while I stretched paycheck after paycheck.

By the end of year five, I informed my father I was going home to Wisconsin to work in his financial services agency. Driving up to my newly sold Minneapolis house with a moving van for our trip back home, he emerged from behind the wheel somewhat incredulous, believing this was something he'd never see his daughter do. But at age twenty-six, I'd had enough of corporate America with its iron-clad restrictions on how and when I worked and how much I could earn. **I was ready to learn how to be my own boss.** Something about being in control of my time and the idea of unlimited earning potential provided ample incentive for me to make the change. I was ready to be in charge of my life.

THE FIRST CUT IS THE DEEPEST— BUT THE REST CAN ALSO HURT!

Most people in the industry will tell you the first three years are the hardest. You get knocked down a lot, or as a woman you tend to knock yourself down just to beat someone else to the punch. The truth is I wanted to give up every single day because of the explosive, evolving amount of material—products and services—that needed to be absorbed and mastered in order to best serve clients and eclipse the competition, of which there is a lot. Things were daunting. I had many doubts. I felt paralyzed. I had a mammoth mountain to climb—one that seemed to grow taller and rockier every day. I didn't think I was capable of doing it. There's a significant learning curve in financial services, and I believed I'd never reach the point where I would be fluent—the way my father was. That was the problem: I believed in my failure—not my success.

Adding to my load was the image I'd had of my father for so long as I was growing up, and continued to have now as a member of his profession—not having a life outside of his job. I reaffirmed to myself that I could not and would not conduct business the way he did. Though I had so much to learn fundamentally, being a cold, hard, brass tacks, "next transaction, please" sales machine wasn't who I was, and barring a radical personality and gender change, it wasn't who I'd ever be. I didn't want it.

On a particularly dark afternoon, I sat in my father's office, boldly confessing my doubts. In fact, I was in tears. But he quickly rose to the challenge and kept me engaged.

"Jules," he said, using the nickname he'd called me since I was a little girl, **"there's a goldmine for you here."**

Financial success withstanding, my father was not referring to money at all that day.

"I see something in you that you don't yet see in yourself," he continued, acknowledging a potential that was not part of my vernacular. He was talking about becoming a success inside—not just on paper. Whether or not I emulated the way he did business, he was talking about creating a life for myself.

§

In a 2011 McKinsey study,[1] men were found to be promoted based on their potential, while women were promoted based on past achievements. Also, I'd read that men and women often view the same job description differently. A man would look at it and say, "I can't do all of this. But I've got 20 percent of it nailed, so I think I can do the job and I'm going to apply." A woman, on the other hand, looks at the same description and says, "I have only 20 percent of the skills they're looking for, so I'm not even going to apply." That's a huge disparity in how we view our potential.

This struck a chord because I recalled the afternoon with my father when I was very close to resigning—perhaps returning to the corporate life that wasn't right for me either. But I didn't know what else to do. I never recognized anything close to potential in me, though my father apparently did. I think a lot of what goes on in our heads as women is a kind

---

[1] *Unlocking the Full Potential of Women at Work.* McKinsey & Company (April 2011). http://www.mckinsey.com/client_service/organization/latest_thinking/unlocking_the_full_potential

of negative self-talk, which I address in depth in Chapter 7, and I had to work hard to expunge those voices that chattered incessantly about my faults and limitations.

Rising to the challenge the way my father had with me, I told him he was right. (I also told him that I thought part of the reason he spoke to me the way he did was that I was the succession plan, as he was preparing to slow down!) But there was no denying he was right about what I could do. There was a goldmine in our industry, and I did have the ability to persevere. In fact, it was a defining moment (see Chapter 10), one in which I made a shift in how I viewed the career choice I'd made three years earlier. **I began to approach my work very differently.** While it wasn't an instantaneous path to loving what I did for a living each day, and there were many bends ahead in the road, I was able to frame it differently in light of the potential my father saw in me—something I was beginning to acknowledge.

With that, I knew if I was going to find success in financial services, it wasn't going to be up to my dad to make me successful. He could provide the tools, encouragement, and some opportunity, but what I did with everything was up to me. It was another defining moment. In a "Success on PURPOSE" talk I give, an aphorism by Theodore Roosevelt to which I often refer best illustrates my actions at the time—and all the time:

"In any moment of decision, the best thing you can do is the right thing, the next best thing is the wrong thing, and the worst thing you can do is nothing."

I had to take responsibility for achieving my own success. I had to do something.

In the twenty years that have followed, I became a trustee to the NAIFA board, a NAIFA secretary, and then in 2014 the organization's first female president. The top of the 40,000-member National Association of Insurance and Financial Advisors became a goal I achieved. Clearly, I was not elected because I was a woman, as I doubt that would have happened. Rather, I was elected because I worked hard at acknowledging my own strengths and capabilities, and had a deep desire to help people. The results manifested in my expanding business and my work for the NAIFA organization, where I focused on responding to members' needs, making the 125-year-old organization more effective in the process.

Believe it or not, the financial services industry really is a helping profession. For pennies on the dollar, you get to provide the solutions that prevent the hardship that comes when a spouse dies, or a business owner does, or a breadwinner is disabled, or someone needs long-term care. You get to keep families and businesses solvent and together in the worst of times.

Women tend to be great listeners, recall a lot of detail, focus on building relationships, and are inherently nurturing, and educating clients about their options is a natural expression of these attributes (see Chapter 2). These and many other elements make financial services a good fit, but again, finding it within yourself to acknowledge, cultivate, and really use these qualities is what will make you a successful advisor.

§

When my parents divorced, my mother entered the life insurance industry in 1986 at a time when women were more or less an oddity in the profession. Unfortunately, even today women make up only 22 percent of affiliated agents and advisors, and in 1986 that figure was 13 percent (LIMRA). As an administrative professional, she'd been told she was overqualified for most of the jobs she sought to return to at the time, but there was a sense of urgency for her to support her family. She jumped into life insurance with both feet a time when the odds of forging her own path—a way of doing business that played to her strengths—were probably not in her favor. But even then, she made the profession her own. In every way, my mother's natural instincts to protect her family translated to male and female clients whose goal was the same. There was no dichotomy of purpose, and in fact I learned from her that life insurance—now generally merged with financial services—is truly a purpose-filled career.

§

My goal in writing this book is to motivate women who are considering the best way to live fully productive, purposeful lives. When you consider the unrelenting demands of earning a living, raising a family, and community involvement, the opportunity to be in charge of your income and your time, and to have these advantages by helping others in the process, is unparalleled.

There is also the myth that financial services is all about numbers. I don't consider myself to be a numbers person. The bulk of my time is spent developing relationships with prospects and clients, educating them about products and services that can serve them in times of tragedy and throughout their lives, and staying abreast of an evolving industry (laws, rules and regulations, viable companies and products) so that I can help them stay current in their choices.

Here are some industry facts and statistics you may want to know:

- According to a 2015 Life Happens/LIMRA Barometer Study, based on 234 million adults age eighteen and older, 43 percent (100 million) have no life insurance.

- Eighty-one percent of U.S. adults say life insurance is something "most people need," but only 38 percent have individual life insurance.

- Thirty percent of partnered/married households wish their spouse/partner would purchase more life insurance.[2]

- And according to a Genworth Lifejacket study, 40 percent of those who have life insurance don't think they have enough.[3]

- Over the next nine or ten years, we'll lose 40 percent of insurance salespeople to retirement. There are currently 300,000 licensed insurance persons in the industry, so 120,000 will be leaving due to death, retirement, and normal attrition.

- Only 15 percent of new hires are retained at the end of four years, meaning we're going to lose 12,000 individuals a year.[4]

- And as mentioned earlier, only 22 percent of affiliated agents and advisors are women—a figure that hasn't changed much in nearly twenty years. There is room and immeasurable opportunity for you.

Women need to understand that they deserve to be at the table. They should be successful. Nothing external should

[2] *Insurance Barometer Study.* Life Happens/LIMRA (2015).
[3] *Getting Over the Gap: The 2012 Lifejacket Study.* Genworth (2012). https://www.genworth.com/dam/Americas/US/PDFs/Consumer/Product/LTC/140122D.pdf
[4] *Agent Production and Retention Report.* LIMRA Research (2008 and 2013).

stop them from attaining that; it's an internal engine that needs to be consistently primed and ignited until it starts on its own—every time.

Later in the book I talk about "bursting moments," or little epiphanies along the way where something you've done clicks and you understand you've made it. You've achieved something significant, which propels you along to the next bursting moment because you carry it with you. It's a feeling that you want to reflect on and replicate over and over again, sipping it from your own snifter of adrenalin.

I can show you how and why financial services is a purpose-driven career that serves you while you serve others.

VALUE ADDED: FUNDS FOR THOUGHT

What deep-seated beliefs do you have about yourself that may be preventing you from achieving your biggest professional (and personal) goals? Where did they come from? Are they gender-based? What immediate and long-term steps can you take to challenge them?

Chapter 2

The Industry Is Set Up for Men, Not for Women—And Why Financial Services Is Actually a Great Field for Women!

JUST AFTER WORLD WAR II, WHEN JAPAN HAD LOST so many of its soldiers, the Japanese government went to great lengths to find employment for its widowed population. Appealing to the country's insurance professionals, the government persuaded the male-dominated industry to hire these women, who had become the sole providers for their families. As it turned out, Japan quickly embraced women as an insurance sales force.

While the industry in Japan is set up differently than it is in the United States, with salaried advisors—rather than independent producers—given a narrow territory and told which product(s) to sell in a specific time period, women drive the sales force and do very well. The profession is considered largely a female domain.

In the United States, financial services training continues to be designed primarily for male advisors. What has been taught is a product-driven, hard-sell process, rather than a protocol that promotes relationship-building through education and more listening, eventually leading to the sale of the product. **The softer sell, which women advisors characteristically favor, may be a slower process, but it's typically a stronger one because it provides for an enduring advisor-client relationship.**

The fact is there are also men who excel at relationship selling. Despite their training, through their own experiences they may have arrived at the conclusion that they are more effective that way, but historically the industry way is more traditionally to get in there, deliver the party line, get the job done, and move on to the next sale.

Since I started in the business twenty years ago, I've seen a positive shift. We're beginning to see more sales training that favors a broader education component with clients, along with more comprehensive fact-finding, more listening, and the spirit of helping people. The listening factor is critical because you can go to a meeting, having studied a company or individual as much as possible ahead of time.

You've decided you know what they need, but then through a kind of diligent, face-to-face intelligence gathering, you do a 90- or 180-degree turn because that deeper exploration of their needs or problems uncovers something other than what you'd anticipated. If you are not predisposed to asking a lot of questions, and then listening between the lines, you may end up prescribing a solution for a problem that really isn't one—a cure for an illness that doesn't exist.

GO FISH (HUNT, OR WAGGLE)

It may be hard to believe, but despite the fact that this is the 21st century, contests, sales incentives, and promotions in the financial services industry are still geared toward men. In the course of a year, the number of company and product incentive contests that cross my desk, where the grand prize is a fishing or hunting trip, or a weekend of golf at a noted resort, is astounding. While I have nothing against fishing, hunting, or golf, chances are I'd be more inclined to participate if I didn't have to go out and invest in a Shimano casting reel, Shilen DGV hunting rifle, or set of Titleist golf clubs, and if the offerings also included a spa day or shopping spree. Again, I know women who love being out in the woods for a few days at a stretch, but many of us would prefer to spend at least some of that time on a massage table or in Neiman Marcus.

Incentives aside, ideas about training are shifting, and while it won't happen overnight, there are options today where if you're just getting into the industry, you can take the time to identify a firm that will allow you to cultivate your own style and use it.

In some of the larger affiliated companies, you're in a "captive" environment where you may have to strictly adhere to a script and check all the boxes with clients. If the track system is not your modus operandi, ask enough questions going in to determine what's required of agents and advisors so you can choose a company that lets you focus on your personality and strengths, not one that winds you up like a toy and sends you in the door.

To attract today's top talent, especially among Gen X and Y, more staid and traditional firms need to modernize their training tenets to accommodate evolving work styles, as this isn't the working world it was thirty, twenty, or even ten years ago. **To be a top producer today, female or male, more times than not you have to be creative in your approach,** and creativity generally involves the freedom to do what works best for you on the path to achieving a goal.

§

When I began my official involvement with NAIFA in 2003 as a trustee on the national board, in the organization's (now 125-year) history, only a handful of women had been trustees. Four women before me had attempted to become secretary, which I did in 2012 when I think the timing was finally right. The stars also apparently aligned in 2014 when I was elected president. And it's been my perception that as women have continued to break through, they have also gotten bolder and more willing to stand up and speak out, make sure their needs are heard and methods employed, and that they are available to mentor other women so that they, too, can be successful.

Around the time of Title IX's passage in 1972, women were often viewed as lone wolves, the mantra being every woman for herself. There was the perception that instead of mentoring one another, typically women saw each other as competition for the few opportunities available to them. That probably wasn't too far from the truth.

This was also because except in rare instances, they'd not had the experience of being on a real team—the kind where members knew how to sit out on the bench for an inning, understanding that through their efforts, when they helped make someone else successful, everybody won.

In my early years with NAIFA, there were highly ambitious, highly successful women advisors, but only in their own, individual worlds. As women became increasingly aware of the bigger picture, and were accepted into leadership roles, they could be passionate, vocal, and make a mark without risking bias or rejection—which could be deleterious to their careers. Just as men do, women have a significant amount of information and experience to bring to the financial services boardroom and it is good to see them coming forward. Can you see yourself there?

FEMALE FIELD OF DREAMS

Eighty-five percent of consumer purchases today are made by women.[1] Statistically women pay the bills, decide what goes into which account, and handle most, if not all, of the family's financial decisions.

I had a new client in my office who didn't bring her husband to our meeting. When I told her we needed to have him with us the next time, she replied that she handled everything, so it really wasn't necessary. I explained that while that was all right to a point, it's important for him to understand why we're taking the course of action we are when it comes to their money. Fifty years ago—maybe even twenty years ago—this never would have happened as she likely would have been the one excluded from a meeting about financial decisions.

My firm has a large family farm client who's been with us for about thirty years, since when my father was still at the helm. The wife does all the financials, and the husband and sons run the operation. When my dad retired, I began to work with them, getting to know them, building a relationship.

[1] "Women Make Up 85% of All Consumer Purchases." Bloomberg. http://www.bloomberg.com/news/videos/b/9e28517f-8de1-4e59-bcda-ce536aa50bd6

In time the wife, who controlled the checkbook of this $15 million family agriculture business, told me that all these years, she'd never fully understood their insurance and investments. That was a problem—until she started working with me.

"You were able to explain things in a way that I got it," she said. "Your dad, as wonderful as he is, seemed to explain it in such a way that my husband could understand. But I could never relate to the information."

Today, we've enrolled them in even more products. I went back in and explained in great detail why we did what we did with them, why we had things set up in a certain way, and provided a spreadsheet to summarize things to which she could readily relate. Now she knows why she's paying a premium and where it's all heading. The details I was able to help provide simplified her life and gave her a greater peace of mind she'd not had before.

As a rule, consumers like to work with an advisor who looks the way they do and speaks their language— literally or figuratively. It's no surprise that this can be true in other professions as well. Psychologists tell us people are simply more comfortable working with someone they perceive as an equal—an individual who is more inclined to understand them. In that respect consumers are driving what we need in the industry. If women are making 85 percent of buying decisions, logic tells us that an automatic connection can be made with other women.

§

Let me reaffirm that though women tend to operate more in the relationship-building realm, clearly there are very successful male advisors who have strong relationship-building skills and use them advantageously in their work. But with women, cultivating people and taking the time to dig out the details tends to be second nature—more or less in their DNA. In the painstaking task of building a business, remembering that someone was remodeling a house after a flood, leaving for Turks and Caicos, or that their child was about to undergo surgery when you ran into them at the store six months ago can go a long way in turning that individual into a client. It's impressive no matter how you look at it. Women more typically are predisposed to acquiring, banking, and months or years later being able to quickly produce these "useless facts," which can turn out to be not so useless in the long run.

Taking that concept one step further, two days before I went to meet with a young couple who were to be new clients, the wife was diagnosed with terminal breast cancer. At the table together we all cried, and I was openly devastated because just by fate I was two days late and they were going to need that coverage. As women we tend to empathize more; we take it in; we internalize; we understand when a family is experiencing pain and hurt; we are nurturers. Characteristically we are more verbal, using lots of words to explain complex and even simple ideas—natural educators to the core. Again, it's not that men cannot do these things; but women seem to be born to it—something that serves advisors immeasurably well in financial services. These kinds of connections to people cement relationships, making them indispensable.

Years ago, I began working as an advisor to a female dentist who worked for a male dentist who was my father's client. She and I immediately connected because we were both young female professionals. We also both bought out our male bosses at about the same time. I continue to serve her in an advisory capacity, but there is more to our relationship. We meet for lunch a few times a year because in financial services it's imperative to stay abreast of the law, evolving rules and regulations, new products, and changes in your clients' lives (she is now married), making sure they are current and appropriately covered.

But our meetings are so much more than that: emblematic of a strong advisor-client relationship. As female business owners, we connect in so many ways and are able to benefit from one another's experiences. One might say we grew up in business together, and whether you represent women business owners, other professionals, career hotel or restaurant workers, or stay-at-home moms, with 85 percent of financial decision-makers being women, opportunities abound for female advisors. It's a great club to belong to, and it's wide open for membership. Energy drinks provided. Don't forget your locker key.

VALUE ADDED: FUNDS FOR THOUGHT

What would you put at the top of your list of natural attributes to help qualify you as a financial advisor? What other qualities do you possess that would underscore your ability for success in this industry?

Chapter 3

The Flexibility Factor: Financial Services Lets You Balance Your Roles Like No Other Career

IN THE WORLD OF NANNY CAMS, LEAFY GREEN FICUS cams, and ultra-surveillance in general, there's probably a cache of footage of me hunched over my computer in my early years in the industry, trying to outdo myself at solitaire.

When I first started in financial services, I used to ask myself what I was going to do that day. After all, I'd left the corporate world and was now in control of my schedule, right? I'd reason that if I didn't have anybody to talk to yet, why not play solitaire! But as the minutes and hours (and, yes, sometimes days) ticked by, I eventually realized I'd have to find something relevant and productive to do—even reading industry journals or other material that would improve my game (the professional one, not the one with kings, queens, jacks, and aces) and stimulate my thought processes. If I wanted success, I had to generate ideas on how to achieve it and apply them. I had to be disciplined in thought and action.

Financial services is a career that offers great flexibility. **You have the opportunity to schedule your work around the rest of your life, rather than the other way around, which is how most careers work.** It's the quintessential work-life balance if you want it, but you have to figure out how to make that concept work for you.

In a 2012 article on *Forbes.com*, which identified a FlexJobs survey, 96 percent of parents said having a traditional full-time job conflicted with caring for their families. Two-thirds reported frequent conflict. In fact, 97 percent of respondents said they believed a flexible position would help them be better parents.[1]

IN THE BEGINNING

With flexibility comes a responsibility to yourself to pull it all together, because as tempting as it may be, working

---

1 Jenna Goudreau. "The 10 Best Jobs for Work and Family Balance." *Forbes* (December 12, 2012). http://www.forbes.com/sites/jennagoudreau/2012/12/12/the-10-best-jobs-for-work-and-family-balance

a few hours a day won't make you successful in financial services. In the beginning—even for the first few years—you may find yourself logging more work hours than you did in another profession because there is so much to learn. It's an intense time when you have to comprehend the products, the process, how to serve clients, and so much more. There are terms and questions and so many other elements you need to master; there are tangibles and intangibles. You have to learn how to understand and sometimes distill what your clients may be telling you to find solutions to their problems. Some of this can be taught, and the rest comes from repeated exposure and experience.

The fact is I became completely discouraged over and over again in those first few years, believing I'd made a terrible mistake. I was ready to rush back to corporate America, where I'd been equally unhappy. But my investment of time and energy—and the kind of epiphany I'd had following that dark afternoon in my father's office (see Chapter 1)—ultimately drove me forward. I finally reached the point where I could begin to let go a little and ease into the flexibility that had drawn me to the industry in the first place.

§

In the realm of flexibility, it's incumbent upon advisors to develop the kind of discipline and time management skills that can give them the freedom they want—the choice to attend a daughter's soccer game at 3 p.m. on a weekday, or take a coveted morning spin class, or take a few days off to tend to an ailing family member. But not at the expense of your future.

If you want to take an hour off to play solitaire (not likely—just saying!) or maybe volunteer for a cause in your community, each of these and a lot more is possible. You're neither punching a clock nor reporting to anyone—except yourself. Sometimes new advisors don't fully understand what's involved in structuring a workday (or evening) so that everything gets done, nothing conflicts with anything else, and there is room for the rest of their lives. **But when they master the art of time management, a life in financial services provides for abundant freedom and fulfillment.**

Many women I know in this industry are moms with young children. They take some time to get their kids off to school and start working at 8:30 or 9 a.m. They stop working at around 3 p.m. to pick them up, help them with homework, feed the family, and get the kids to bed. Then they sit down to make client calls in the evening until 8:30 or 9 p.m., perhaps study new laws or products, or prepare for tomorrow's appointments after that. Evenings are also a great time to reach clients and prospects at home when they are not bandied about by deadlines, pressures, and time constraints at their places of business. **Female advisors can blend their work into their lives, or their lives into their work.**

Again, while the industry's flexibility factor is hugely attractive, it doesn't imply complete freedom. You cannot invest only a few hours a day, a few days a week, and expect to cross the finish line. But if you develop the right kind of work skills, the potential to have it all—or something very close—is there.

When I worked in corporate America, my hours at the bank were from 8 a.m. to 5 p.m. I had to be there during those hours, at my desk, in my seat. Sometimes I worked longer and late, or through lunch, or came in early—which was not reflected in my salary. Hard, long, extra work did not imply an increase in income that week or month—the way it can when you are in control of your life in financial services. But whatever else I did at the bank, I had to be at my desk from 8 to 5, no matter what.

I also had a fixed amount of vacation time, which was two weeks per year when I started out and then eventually three weeks. When you think about it, that's not a lot of time in a fifty-two-week year. I'm a card-carrying world traveler and knew at some point I wanted to take some extensive trips that may require more time. While I wasn't juggling raising a family vis-à-vis work at that point, nevertheless I wanted to broaden my scope, enrich my life, and learn as much as possible in a different locale. A big part of the reason I left the corporate world was that being in charge of my own life was important to me. In financial services,

31

if I plan for a trip, I have the option of working increased hours and more days prior to my departure so that I know my clients are covered, I don't lose time and steps in working to generate new business, and I feel comfortable taking the time away—whatever reasonable period of time I want.

§

Several years ago, my mother—the life insurance agent I referenced in the previous chapter—had cancer. It was her third time battling the disease. She had to undergo radiation treatment five days a week for five weeks. Because of the flexibility in this industry, I was able to arrange my schedule around taking her to every appointment. I'd go into the office first and begin my workday, leave to pick her up for the ten- to fifteen-minute drive to the facility, sit with her during the fifteen-minute procedure, and then take her home to my house where she was staying. Had I not been in a profession that provided this kind of flexibility, I'd have had to hire someone to drive her back and forth. Though it was a challenge to take this kind of bite out of my daily schedule, I'd not have had the opportunity to care for her in the same way she had always been there for me. Being able to accompany her during treatment was something important to both of us. It's that precious time you have together when someone you love is sick that you can never get back.

Success comes in many forms. If I could have been in my office during that time, seeing clients for forty or fifty hours a week, I'd likely have found more financial success. But I also knew in that moment of my mother's illness that success to me was making sure I spent time with her—even if it meant I wasn't going to generate the kind of financial rewards I might have under other conditions.

As God would have it, my mother has been cancer-free for quite a while. But even when she was sick, because she was also in the industry and in control of her work schedule, she didn't lose her job. This industry gave both of us everything we needed at a very challenging time. It continues to provide opportunities for us as my seventy-plus-year-old mom still carries that big briefcase she's worked so hard to fill. She's semi-retired, making her own hours and choosing the days she will work, gainfully serving her long list of clients.

LOCATION LOCATION LOCATION

Okay—so the above is a real estate colloquialism, but it aptly applies to financial services as well. For many advisors, when success becomes something they can really measure, escaping the cold, perhaps spending more time around relocated family, or possibly just wanting to enjoy a different part of the country prompts them to acquire a second home.

An advisor in my orbit has an office in Denver and one in Scottsdale to escape the snowy winters, the latter a home office with a view. As a rule he meets with all of his clients virtually—from wherever he is. Toward the end of his career, my father did the same, summering in the Midwest and also wintering in Arizona. In financial services, obtaining registrations and licensure in other states (though different products and services require different registrations/licenses) allows you to set up shop anywhere, anytime, as the only clock you are punching is the internal one and the only desk you are required to be at is the one in front of you at the moment—the one you have chosen.

While Baby Boomers and the ones that preceded them lived to work, my generation and the one that came after us, Gen Xers and Millennials, work to live. We seek to fashion our lives—family, community involvement, sports, travel, and other elements—around how we support ourselves, and the main ingredient in the flexibility strategy involved here is time management.

To get your feet wet in the industry, there is also the option to start at a smaller firm as an assistant or paraplanner, where one is exposed to inner industry workings but with more traditional hours and maybe a salary or hourly rate. Though flexibility may need to be postponed for a while, this provides a more consistent, steady stream of income while you learn the business. Financial services is about commission sales, and for some it is a leap of faith to jump right in. Working as an assistant or paraplanner gives you time for a financial services on-the-job education, time to get your registrations and licenses, and then when you are ready you can move into sales.

§

When I became president of NAIFA and my workload essentially doubled, my flexible schedule increased to seven days a week. It was a choice that worked for me as it can for others who are juggling burgeoning components of their lives. In my case I knew it would only be for a year.

In a more corporate environment, such as the bank I used to work at, I did not have the luxury of intertwining life and work that I have now. During the year of my NAIFA presidency, I may have been watching a Packers game on a Sunday, replying to the fifty to one hundred emails I got each day, and catching up with clients (with young families or the middle-income market, nights and weekends at home is a good time and place to find them), but it was all doable. It was all by design and I knew then, as I do every day, that I made the right decision in choosing a career in financial services.

§

Do you have a life full of plans and possibilities you'd like to enjoy, or develop more, and/or have the time to cultivate more outside interests? Are you pulled in a thousand directions, trying to fit your family time into a limited number of evening and weekend hours, sometimes relegating it to the back burner—something you promised yourself you'd never do? Do you have laser-sharp focus so that in a more flexible job, when you are working in a designated time period, you are completely present and not allowing for distractions (some call it the ability to compartmentalize)? These are important considerations for a good fit in the flexible world of financial services.

VALUE ADDED:
FUNDS FOR THOUGHT

What elements of your life right now would you like to change? Do you have the flexibility today to create a work-life balance exactly as you need and want it to be? What would it take for you to be able to do that in your current career without parts of your personal and professional day, week, month, and year coming up short?

Chapter 4

Women Make Great Leaders, Too

"If your actions inspire others to dream more,
learn more, do more, and become more, you are a leader."
—John Quincy Adams

W HEN WE THINK OF INFLUENTIAL LEADERS, PROB-
ably more times than not men come to mind first. And
though John Quincy Adams's words were conceived in a
time when women, with few exceptions, generally were not
"allowed" to lead, the sixth U.S. president's keen observation
is not gender-specific.

It applies to many thousands of individuals, female and
male, throughout history and throughout the world. These
leaders have masterfully guided others through and out of
often incomprehensible situations toward brighter days.

Solution-oriented leaders are imbued with traits many of us emulate, thinking we may not have what it takes. But as a woman, you'd be surprised at the qualities you naturally possess that enable you to mobilize a group, build and empower a staff, and lead a reticent, uncertain, or skeptical client to the most effective solution for their problem. While that is not to say men don't possess some or all of these characteristics in one form or another, these qualities provide the foundation for leadership in the financial services industry.

Historically, and certainly in contemporary times, when we consider female leaders such as Margaret Thatcher, Golda Meir, Eva Peron, Condoleezza Rice, Facebook COO and author Sheryl Sandberg, Yahoo CEO Marissa Mayer, Carly Fiorina, and others, what often stands out is a strong presence and sense of control. Does this come from extraordinary achievement? Perhaps. **But long before each woman had established a track record, she must have acknowledged something deep inside that provided the self-confidence to pursue her goals and obtain those achievements—no matter what.** And what about Anne Frank? In her diary, a young girl demonstrated an incisive and indelible faith in human nature despite the atrocities of war. That, too, is a leadership quality: the ability to see in people what others may not. Early on, my father saw in me what I hadn't even seen in myself (see Chapter 1). Though our business philosophies differ, I have always considered him a great leader.

So what are the qualities women seem to come by naturally that make them exceptional leaders?

DO YOU HEAR WHAT I HEAR?

Women typically have a black belt in listening. While I know men who do it well, the difference is women tend to listen with the intent to understand, where men often listen in order to speak—to use what they hear as a prelude to "What am I going to say next?" Women have a knack for taking in and digesting what they're hearing to utilize not necessarily at that moment, but to add to their mental storehouse of what I call "useless facts." These useless facts turn out to be not so useless (see Chapter 2) as they are in your mental storehouse, ready to be applied to something relevant in the future—something that may garner a new client. Can you recall a time you ran into someone you hadn't seen in months or even years, but who remembered from your last conversation that you were going back to school for another degree, or that your son was about to undergo arthroscopic surgery for a sports injury? Impressive, wasn't it? And it certainly racks up points in the relationship-building department.

Also in the context of listening, women have a penchant for empathy. They are known to project themselves into the shoes of the speaker, which is an important quality, especially when dealing with a challenging situation. Diplomacy and finding an acceptable solution are a lot easier when empathy is present.

HARMONIOUS DISCORD

There are times when enmity (or worse) reigns, and despite that, women seem to be great consensus builders. I have always had a personal objective not to leave a room stomping and angry, and to make sure others don't either. My goal is to get everybody to understand each other and then come to a conclusion that the group can get behind. Frankly, there isn't a lot of it in Washington, but that's another conversation.

When we listen well, and empathize, consensus building is a natural progression, and many women have an inherent ability to pull factions together. Again, it's not to say that men can't do this, but in my twenty years in the industry, I've seen women advisors instinctively and effectively take the time to educate clients, office staff, and others, ultimately producing better-informed people (even former adversaries) around them, as they involve them in the decision-making process. There's nothing like joint ownership of a decision to create a cohesive group.

TAKING RELATIONSHIP-BUILDING TO TASK

There may be a danger of lapsing into stereotypes here, but because women in the workplace have traditionally had to juggle work, family, and household chores for generations, and many single moms (and, yes, some single dads) do it today, women have evolved into exceptional multitaskers. This goes along with women's facility for remembering those seemingly useless facts, which once again turn out to be not so useless and which make people feel good and are real relationship-builders. I don't think women are better or worse at relationship-building than men, but as nurturers, they go about it in a different way.

When I was appointed to the board of trustees of NAIFA, I built longstanding, mutually beneficial relationships that I was able to call upon in becoming secretary and to help me attain the highest office I could: NAIFA president. Because I'd invested a lot of time in genuinely getting to know everything I could about the people with whom I came in contact, they helped vote me into office and I could also count on them to help me get things accomplished in a leadership role.

SENSITIVITY GAINING

Much has been debated about the merits or caveats of sensitivity. Boxer Mike Tyson once claimed that his biggest weakness was that he was too sensitive, where others have claimed being sensitive to the needs of others has made them more powerful, effective, and successful.

I'm convinced sensitivity is important and is a close relative of empathy. Women feel things deeply, and sometimes that turns to great passion, as in "I feel so strongly about this

I'm going to go out and get it—no matter what." Conversely, sometimes women have strong feelings about things that are so deeply rooted it turns them sour or points them in the wrong direction. If you are going to be a leader in whatever you do, you need to allow for disappointment and turns that you didn't expect. You need to allow all that—but use it to fuel your passion and keep you on course.

PRESERVE AND PROTECT

In the movie *The Blind Side*, though challenged in almost every way because of his impoverished background, Michael Oher tested exceedingly high in protective instincts. Once these were properly channeled, they made him the proverbial force to be reckoned with on high school and college football teams. He led them to victory and ended up in professional football.

Females of most all species come by their protective instincts naturally, charged with protecting and preserving their babies, perpetuating their respective species. I view this as a leadership quality. Have you ever inadvertently walked beneath a tree in spring where bird's eggs gestated in a nest? Have you been "dive bombed" by the mother?

I am extremely protective of my staff. If I have a client who steps over the line—and the longer you are in business, the chances of this happening increase—I have asked that client to find another financial services office. That kind of thing happens very rarely, but as a leader, you need to be the one out front, and women's natural protective instincts impel them in that regard. When I was president of NAIFA, a member of the NAIFA staff was compromised at one point by an individual's conduct and I quickly made it clear to him that his behavior was not allowed. A leader is the one who has to be out front, not only motivating the team behind her but also acting as a buffer from the outside world. Protecting those who rely on you from abuse or negativity that can derail their work is part of a leader's legacy. As a woman, you naturally possess this instinct.

Clients purchase life insurance and financial services products to help protect their families, assets, and businesses. As a female advisor, the desire to protect is a common thread and goal between you and your clients, enabling you to lead them in the often confusing decision-making process through a blend of products. Again, it's not that men don't possess this attribute in varying degrees. In my experience, it seems to be in women's DNA and makes them highly effective.

SEVERAL STORIES UP

If you've ever spent time coaxing and cajoling a small child to eat, go to sleep, take her medicine, stop screaming, pick up a mess, or get in the car, you probably have a cache of stories up your sleeve. I don't mean the retelling of the feat, but rather the stories you used to get the child to perform the task in the first place. Leaders tend to be great storytellers, as stories explain and illuminate the reasons behind an action or recommendation better than anything. Stories allow people to identify with what's being said.

Women are natural storytellers. When meeting with clients in the financial services industry, storytelling is a vital part of illustrating how and why specific services and products are as effective (or ineffective) as they are, and why they are germane to the client's problem. Stories compel a client to take action based on the passion and urgency communicated by the advisor about how important it is to protect what they have—and whom they love.

A couple that has four children sat in my office one evening with a "reasonable" amount of life insurance already in place. The wife makes more than the husband, and as we sat and talked, I proposed a significant amount of additional coverage for her.

"I'd be insured for an awful lot," was her response.

I explained to her that she is worth a lot, and if something happened to her, the husband would be left juggling four children as a single parent and very likely have to take on a second job just to maintain their standard of living—hiring people to help raise the kids.

"You're right," the wife said after a particularly compelling story I told the couple. "In fact, I'd rather see him be able to cut back on his hours to be with our children at such a time."

This story was as compelling to me as it was to them, maybe more, as it involved my cousin, Sam McNeely.

Sam, an ex-football player at 6 foot 3 inches tall and more than 300 pounds, towered over everyone who came in contact with him. Those who knew him say he was an imposing figure, but with a heart as big as he was. I can underscore that, having known him my entire life.

Within a year of Sam marrying Amy, the couple discovered they were going to be parents. While Sam had some life insurance through his work, Amy convinced him to purchase an individual policy that would help give him sufficient coverage and wouldn't disappear if he changed jobs. Amy got coverage as well.

"If something happened to me, I didn't want to leave him with a child and struggle with work and finding someone to take care of her," she'd said of her decision to purchase her own coverage—and of her urging her husband to increase his coverage.

Several years later, as Amy walked their daughter to school, she received a call that changed her life. Sam was in the hospital with an aortic dissection. Shortly after arriving, it would claim his life. He was thirty-eight.[1]

---

1 "Amy McNeely: Protection Is Paramount." http://www.lifehappens. org/videos/protection-is-paramount

The coverage has helped allow her to be there for their daughter instead of having to work full-time (or more) and find people to care for her.

I've been at the kitchen table delivering a claim check to families who had enough life insurance and some who didn't. The conversation in each case is very different. One takes the financial burden completely off the table, and the other brings it immediately to the top of the list—at a time when the journey through emotional pain is so intense nothing should have to supersede it. But a lack of finances almost has to. In educating clients, real life stories provide powerful reasons to take the actions an advisor may recommend, and women are accomplished in this realm, adding to their leadership potential.

TEAM SPIRIT

If you take a close look, many if not most of the casting directors in Hollywood are women. Women have a proclivity for casting great teams—for aptly filling roles so the result is a TV program or film that works. Maybe paramount to Hollywood, great leaders—politicians, CEOs, religious leaders—have the knack for assembling strong teams of individuals who can accomplish what the leader alone cannot. No one can know or do everything, and a real leader is the first to acknowledge that.

I'm the first to admit I'm not good at everything. I have tried to build a team of people around me who are better at the things I'm not. This includes office staff (support and other advisors) as well as outside experts who may bring specialties to the table we don't have if I need to call on them to help me acquire a specific client.

Doing that has allowed me to extend my reach, generate more business, and find more success. But I still have to lead that team. And it's all-encompassing. You're establishing a larger group than if you did it alone, and together you're finding success.

Men certainly do this, and women are undeniably equal to the task of team building—a strong leadership quality.

When I took over my father's practice in 2010, there were three people on staff. We currently have six team members in house, and our extended team of professionals nearly doubles that number. I also had to build my NAIFA team while in office.

I always say if you're a leader with no followers—no team behind you—you're just taking a walk. And while we've established that women communicate well and are great storytellers, they also have a natural ability to harness the variety of talented individuals out there that will help propel them down that road to success.

§

If you've never thought about the leadership qualities within you, and even if you have but weren't sure how to galvanize and apply them, test driving them in the financial services industry is an opportunity to build a career on what comes naturally. To quote Arianna Huffington, "We cannot wait for a leader to ride in on a white horse to save us. We all need to find the leader in the mirror."

VALUE ADDED: FUNDS FOR THOUGHT

Think back to those circumstances in your life when, as an employee, daughter, sister, wife, mother, friend, volunteer, or other, you wanted to or had to take the lead. Was it a struggle or did it come naturally? Did you feel a sense of accomplishment afterward? Would you like to implement more of it in your life?

Chapter 5

Why Women Function Better
With a Team

TEAMS ARE A CRITICAL COMPONENT OF SUCCESSFUL advisors. In Chapter 4, I talked about team building as a strong characteristic of leaders and how adept women are at assembling talented teams who have the potential to work well together and advance the group as a whole. Also, because women are inherently good communicators and listeners, working on a team allows them to exercise those qualities frequently.

But what exactly constitutes a team, and why do women function better with them, whether they're out in front and have put one together or are a valued member of one—or both?

First, I'm on several teams. My primary team comprises other advisors and support staff. It's my practice, and I have an extended team of individuals (other advisors with their own areas of knowledge, skill, or experience) to whom I can reach out when I have issues with clients that are not within the realm of my specialty. I could not be fully successful in this industry without them. There are tasks I'm quite accomplished at doing and others I'm not, so it's also important to surround myself with people who have different orientations and/or the time to do things I don't because of my other responsibilities.

I have someone who completes and processes paperwork, and tracks business through the pipeline. Someone else sets up and preps for appointments, based on my direction. I know advisors who have research teams that explore different investment choices and do all the modeling and more in that arena. There are many ways to design your team, and again I'm certain that I could not have functioned nearly as well without mine—certainly not without my NAIFA team and volunteers—especially during the year I was NAIFA president and traveling a lot.

My other team is my study group. I cannot stress enough how important it is to connect with a group of like-minded individuals. In my case, we are five women financial advisors, spread all over the country. We have structured face-to-face meetings with set agendas a few times a year. **These women are an integral part of my success.** We share everything about our practices. We talk through goals and employee issues. We talk through anything with which we're not comfortable, hoping to glean information in the process.

With the right group, these individuals become trusted confidantes on whom you can call when a client situation is out of your typical wheelhouse. We hold each other accountable for what was promised in the first quarter, for example, or what we may have identified as an additional direction for our respective companies. The depth and scope of information, and the overall support this team of peers provides on so many levels, are unparalleled. You might say we function as each other's resource library, sounding board, suggestion box, safety net when necessary—and so much more. There is great value for each of us in being a member of this extraordinary team.

§

The financial services industry is constantly evolving, becoming far more complex than ever with a plethora of products. Teaming today is more expected and accepted by clients than it was thirty years ago when my mother started in the insurance industry, or even twenty years ago when I joined my father's practice. There are advisors who specialize in life insurance, health insurance, long-term care, retirement planning, and more—each specialty having a wealth of complexities, changing laws, and rules and regulations attached to them.

I'm a full financial planner with a broad scope of experience or knowledge, but I can't specialize in everything or I'd spread myself too thin. And let's be frank, in the working world we tend to excel at what we're passionate about, so it's best to focus on those things. I always say if I'm standing outside a burning building, next to a firefighter, why would I attempt to run in and rescue someone when there's a trained professional just steps away who is better qualified to do that? That's the real concept behind teaming.

I had a contractor client who'd not had a financial advisor in the past. During our initial meeting, it became clear that he was excellent at his trade, but he was really struggling at running his expanding business. Though I could provide the financial planning that was warranted at that point, I could not wear all the hats he needed to get his arms around his growing business.

Because I believe in teams that have worked so well for me, I immediately set about harnessing one for him. He had a bookkeeper, but the business had grown to the point where he needed the support of a CPA, which I recommended. I also connected him with one of the attorneys on my extended team as there were documents that needed to be drafted: a will, trust, power of attorney, healthcare power of attorney. It was a time in the client's life where he needed to move from sole proprietor to an LLC. The team I brought in enabled him to take control of his business and keep his focus on what he did best, without becoming bogged down in what he didn't. The team made it comfortable, enjoyable, and manageable for my client again, and with an eye toward helping him take his business to the next level.

§

Growing up, I had the advantage of playing on sports teams. But before the 1972 passage of Title IX—a comprehensive federal law that prohibits discrimination on the basis of sex in any federally funded education program or activity—women were often excluded from them. The popular thinking was that, as girls became grown women, because of the deficit of team experience, fewer women learned the tenets of teamwork, such as how to sit out temporarily and let someone more qualified take over for the good of the team (taking one for the team, so to speak).

Also, in previous decades there were so few jobs of merit for women that competition for the token openings or quotas (remember affirmative action?) was keen, and women may have seen one another as the enemy rather than colleagues with shared interests and concerns, worthy of mutual support and encouragement. Fortunately that has changed.

My experience in this industry is that women want to nurture, support, and when appropriate mentor other women—and colleagues of both genders, for that matter. My comfort level in putting together a team for my contractor client was a result of having built relationships with members of this team. I could count on them, assured they would have the same regard for my client as I did. **Teams also provide a real service to the client in the communications arena as they are set up so that things don't fall through the cracks.** Sometimes clients come in with one of their own in place, but other times they don't know exactly where to turn and this can slow down the process, even leaving important elements undone. If they turn to you for recommendations, it's always good to have one of your own to share.

NO WOMAN IS AN ISLAND

Many new advisors today try to do it all themselves. When they start out in the industry, hiring a support person is something they put off for economic reasons. **But I advocate investing in someone even before you think you can afford them; an assistant will help you grow your business more quickly and will essentially pay for their own salary if you train them properly.**

When I started in financial services, my father was the sole financial advisor in his practice, along with administrative help from one support person and my stepmom. In time he and my stepmom made the semi-retirement pilgrimage to Arizona six months of the year, leaving me alone with the support person, who was invaluable as I strived to expand the practice. When I achieved that goal, it was time to hire more staff, but in an interesting turn of events, the support person who'd been there for more than a decade wasn't comfortable with the idea, finding it difficult to function. After my father left, she had grown accustomed to a two-person office, so try as I might to work it out, I had to let her go.

Part of the dynamics of team function is making sure you put together a cohesive group—one with shared values. While individualism and creativity are certainly to be prized and encouraged, working together for a common goal—staying strong on the income-producing path—is paramount. As someone in a hiring position, it's important to look for employees with a history of working well within the parameters of a team. That's not to say someone who has worked primarily alone can't adapt, and may be willing to do so given the right environment, but as an employer this has been a red flag to me.

On the other side, when starting out in the industry and interviewing for a position, there are things you can look for to ascertain whether there's a strong team in place that you can become a viable member of.

One of the questions I would ask is if the team leader has a clear vision of where everyone is going—and what that vision is. I'd want to know if the employer had thoroughly assessed the fit of the existing team members—and how your personality and work experience would fit into all that. If possible, it's always good to have an opportunity to talk with the team prior to accepting a job offer.

In my practice, the second phase of the interview process for a new employee is a team interview where everyone sits around the table and gets to ask questions of the candidate—and vice versa. While nothing is guaranteed, it's as close as anything can be to ensuring we make the right hiring decision. And for you, as a job candidate, if a possibility like this exists, it's an opportunity to assess the working environment to make sure it's what you want.

CHECKS AND BALANCES

It's not uncommon in most businesses to have staff meetings, and as women tend to be good communicators and relationship builders, these forums are of particular value. My office has a quick twenty-minute staff meeting every Monday morning where we check in about the week ahead—who's got appointments, pending business, and which clients are coming in—to make sure everybody's on the same page. If anything needs to be done in the way of preparation, we can anticipate and handle it right away then rather than frantically on the day of the meeting.

At the end of each day, we have a protocol where each member of the team emails a sheet to everyone else outlining what they got done that day: clients talked to, follow-up calls and tasks for the next day, what's pending for the next few days. We also meet for an extended ninety-minute monthly meeting where we delve into marketing, additional projects, and anything of a more strategic or time-consuming nature.

Once a year, we have a meeting where our business plans are written and shared.

In this way, we are truly working as a team, supporting one another, driving one another on when necessary, and making sure nothing falls through the cracks.

Finally, when you really think about it, most of us have been an important part of a team since we were born. I always had a job as a kid. It might have been something simple like cleaning the bathrooms or mowing the lawn, but if I didn't contribute to the running of the household, the "home" team wouldn't have functioned as optimally as it could. I was brought up with the concept that everybody in the family has a job, which contributes to the whole and which exposed me to the merits of teamwork. I can't say enough that however you structure yours, a team is an essential component of a successful advisor.

VALUE ADDED:
FUNDS FOR THOUGHT

What skills and experiences have you brought to, or derived from, any teams of which you've been a part in the past? Think about the current teams in your life (and, no, I don't mean the Green Bay Packers!). Do they help empower you, and if so, in what ways? What qualities do you bring to them? How do they help you be more effective at what you do?

Chapter 6

Transitioning Your Practice: Why Are There So Few Mother–Daughter Teams in Financial Services?

For FOURTEEN YEARS I WAS PART OF A FATHER-daughter team. I suspect that in terms of succession planning in the male-dominated financial services industry, the most common arrangement is father-son. It wasn't until I officially took over my father's practice in 2010 that I began to think about mother-daughter teams—wondering how many there were.

When I speak at conferences and events, I talk about second-generation advisors, asking for a show of hands to see how many there are in the room. Invariably a lot of male hands go up as they tell me they're poised to take over their fathers' practices. I'm estimating that 5 to 10 percent of the hand raisers are women, but in almost every instance, they're also taking over their father's practice—not their mother's.

Because financial services is largely still the new frontier for women advisors, and given the fact that a 2014 LIMRA and National Underwriter Life & Health study tells us that only 22 percent of advisors are female,[1] mother-daughter teams are more of a novelty than anything else. They just haven't had a chance to happen. But I aim to help change that.

In my firm, there are three financial representatives and one insurance specialist, with three of the four being women. That's because I try hard to encourage more and more women to choose this career, which in turn will create more mother-daughter teams in the future. In my case, though she may not know it yet, I hope to pass the baton to my niece who will soon be starting college and majoring in business.

When I entered the industry, I chose my father's practice over what my mother was doing because he owned his business and would have absolute control over who his

---

[1] Carly Meiners. "Women: On How to Be Successful and Improve Client Relationships." *LifeHealthPro* (October 6, 2015). http://www.lifehealthpro. com/2015/10/06/women-on-how-to-be-successful-and-improve-client-r

successor was. But my mother became a huge part of how I learned about the industry. I was getting the formal training I needed from my father, as a financial services business owner, but I relied on my mother a lot in that as women we shared the working style and qualities elaborated on in previous chapters.

I also believe that the reason I had a strong desire to surround myself with an all-female study group was because we could relate to one another, offering understanding and encouragement about our trajectories in financial services. We are each other's sounding boards and role models, just as my mother has always been for me—even as she phases out of the industry.

Whatever the gender, business succession, or transitioning from one generation to the next, is never easy—for either the senior or junior advisor. My father used to refer to McNeely Financial Services as his "baby," and whenever the time came for us to make a major (or sometimes even minor) decision about finances, equipment, staff, protocols, or anything else, the conversation usually defaulted to the "but it's my baby" speech.

In many ways I brought the practice into the 21st century, as my dad had come up in the industry doing everything manually. I recall one particularly challenging time when a lingering disagreement over a piece of technology became the defining moments of my week visiting him in the Southwest.

In the late 1990s, I wanted to purchase a significant new server for our Wisconsin office that would allow us to work from anywhere, taking the practice to the next level. It was winter and my dad was spending six months in Arizona. On the first day of my time with him, I pitched him the six-thousand-dollar idea.

Because he was adamant about it not happening, I decided I was going to make it a daily ritual until I got a yes answer. So every single day I prepared my speech, telling him exactly why we needed it—the features and benefits—to which he continued to say no. On the very last day he gave in, saying if it meant that much to me, I should go ahead and get it.

I'm not sure if I wore him down, but when he gave me the "but it's my baby" line again that last time (just before relenting), I told him I definitely understood, and at the same time, it was about to become *my* baby!

"If you're going to take this practice and expand and grow it, making it all it deserves to be, you've got to trust me," I told him.

In order for transitions to work, a high level of trust must develop between the senior and junior advisor. It doesn't happen overnight, but rather through months and even years of open dialogue and consistent performance.

In the three years before my father's retirement, he wanted me to start putting all of my commissions into the business and taking over more responsibility. I told him I was happy to do that, but my concern at that point was that I had no ownership. My thinking was that if I were highly instrumental in building a larger practice that I'd be faced with purchasing in the future, I needed security now. Proposing 51 percent so that I had the ability to make decisions, my father nearly choked. We agreed on a 50/50 split, which gave me at least half ownership, so we had to agree on expenditures and other decisions. We learned to work together that way. My father saw that I was serious, passionate, and dedicated. He saw that I was committed to making the practice as successful as it could be, and that's the point at which he began to really trust me.

For the first six to eight months of our new arrangement, my father wanted me to produce all the financial reports at the end of each month for his perusal. But one day he called me, saying, "You've got this." No more reports. He was able to let go with absolute confidence.

While I acknowledge it was a great challenge for him to pass the mantle, I sometimes think about what would be happening in my own process of turning over this company to someone. Would it be any easier? I don't believe it's ever easy. In some families there could be issues with the family dynamic, but more often than not, with a family member or another successor, it's a matter of trust. It's incredibly difficult, complicated, frightening, and *emotional* to take something that's been your passion—your proverbial blood, sweat, and tears for decades—and just let go.

Regardless of who a seasoned advisor identifies as a successor, it's important to share the wealth of information and all this amazing career has to offer with someone who can be a real asset to the industry. I learned from my mother that she had a deep compassion for her clients. I never had the expectation I would build such strong relationships with clients that they'd become like family to me, but that's something I learned from my mom.

My dad also had strong client relationships, but they were on a different level—perhaps not quite as deep, intimate, or familial. Women tend to have a deeper connection, predicated on the natural ability to empathize, nurture, educate, and all the other reasons outlined in previous chapters. I've cried with my clients, as did my mother. I've been overcome with joy for clients when things go startlingly well in their lives, and they often let me know because they're certain I'll experience these occurrences the same way they do.

If you are a single mom, as is my mother, or the daughter of one, as I am, your bond may be particularly strong. My mom was my lifeline from the time I was a young adolescent. She was the one with whom I lived. She was the one I always went to because I saw her take a difficult situation, rise above it, and find success. She inspired me to the core—over and over. I saw her overcome great obstacles, and that was exactly what I needed to reference a thousand times in my life. I still do.

In addition to my mom, my older sister, and study group, along the way I've acquired mentors and other individuals (women and men) who could also help me get what I needed at particular junctures. Each has generously contributed what they know, and therefore has been invaluable to me, further molding me into the kind of financial services professional my father considered trust- and transition-worthy.

I always say that if women can duplicate themselves, that would be a huge boost in moving things forward—increasing the presence of women advisors and the opportunity for mother-daughter teams for succession in the industry.

Of course, there are always the caveats, or more positively put, the trials of working with a close relative—female or male. Sometimes knowing them extremely well (or thinking you do) can introduce its own set of challenges, such as bringing a not-so-pleasant history into the workplace or being unable to see the other as a businessperson the way others do. Experts say this can be solved in many ways, including not referring to one another as "mom," "honey," or other terms of endearment, which can have a patronizing effect in the office, or by the adult child's nickname. Establishing a set of ground rules—essentially building a new structure where the familiar is subordinated and the professional scenario is given an opportunity to take root—is a good formula for success: the root of the word *succession*, incidentally!

Transitioning takes time, but in this respect the process can't begin until there are more mother-daughter teams in the financial services industry. The November 2015 issue of *InsuranceNewsNet* reports that a decline in agents and advisors will start in 2020 due to a major uptick in anticipated retirement. It goes on to say the industry needs to focus on recruiting and grooming new talent.[2]

The industry is clearly wide open for new advisors. Mothers and daughters have everything it takes to excel in this profession. Let's get started!

VALUE ADDED: FUNDS FOR THOUGHT

Do transitions come easily for you? Are (or were) you part of a family business that had to confront some or all of the issues in this chapter in its succession planning? Even if your daughter(s) are young and it's years down the road, can you see yourself building a powerful business with an eye to your future and theirs in which they could join you?

---

[2] Linda Koco. "Advisor Headcount Ticks Up but a Decline Looms." *InsuranceNewsNet* (November 2015). http://insurancenewsnet.com/innarticle/2015/11/23/advisor-headcount-ticks-upward-but-a-new-decline-is-looming.html

Chapter 7

Saying No to the
Negative Voices in Your Head

WOMEN HAVE ISSUES WITH SELF-ESTEEM. FROM my perspective, it seems to be a constant battle. Earlier, we talked about the fact that a man and a woman can look at the same job description and have very different reactions. The woman might say, "Oh, I only have 20 percent of those skills or requirements, so I don't think I should apply for the job." A man could look at that job description and say, "Oh, I only have 20 percent of what they're asking for, but I know I can do this job, so I'm going to apply."

I don't know if it's genetic, but it seems to be a kind of biological roadblock in female brains that causes them to doubt their abilities to do new things. The more confident you become, the less frequently you have to fight that sense of doubt. Confidence comes from success, so the question I'd like to address in this chapter is this: How do you overcome that sense of self-doubt to give you the sense of confidence to move forward more easily in whatever you're doing?

For myself, in my own career, I noticed that sense of self-doubt was constant. I would tell myself things like, "I can't go out and meet with that client because I don't have enough information on what they're going to ask me about." Or "I can't learn about that new product—I've never looked at it before. It's completely foreign to me." I found myself constantly doubting my ability. I have a lot more confidence in my abilities today, but it's taken twenty years for me to get there. My leadership position in the industry today, and all the work I've done over all these years, has helped build my confidence as a financial advisor and a leader. **The more I build that confidence, the less those negative voices become active in my brain.** So let's talk about how to overcome them.

Tell me if this isn't true for you. At the moment you have that flash of self-doubt, when you tell yourself you're not capable of accomplishing a given task, there's another voice inside of you that says, "I can do anything." Am I right? If so, then I think you're like most women in this regard. So the question is about how to make the "I can do anything" belief stronger than the disbelief about what you're actually capable of. So it's a balancing act, where you're trying to squelch the "I don't believe in myself" voice with the "I can do anything" voice.

One of the first things that helped me was to use motivational quotes. I'm a big believer in those quotes, and I would pick out my favorites and say them over and over in my head when I needed motivation to truly believe in myself. Sometimes I didn't even believe anything I was reading in a quote I was using to motivate myself. I knew, however, that if I said it over and over enough, I would start to believe it. And I did.

One of the quotes I like is **"Action conquers fear."** At times I felt almost paralyzed by the fear that I would never get my arms around all the material I needed to know so that I could go out and serve my clients. The fear would freeze me in my tracks—that's how real it was. But I learned that action can conquer fear. **The only way I was able to overcome my fears was to face those fears.** So it became really huge for me early on to just tell myself, "I'm going to get out there. I'm going to get in front of someone, and if nothing good comes of it, so be it. The good that will come of it, at a minimum, is that I will be out there." That became my mantra early on.

The other quote, and I mentioned this earlier, is from Theodore Roosevelt: **"In any moment of decision, the best**

thing you can do is the right thing, the next best thing is the wrong thing, and the worst thing you can do is nothing." That speaks very clearly about how I felt earlier in my career. I remember thinking that the worst thing I could do is nothing. If I sit at this desk and do nothing, I'm not going to get myself where I want to be. So I was able to overcome my inner struggle by reminding myself that even if I go out and do the wrong thing, it's better than doing nothing. I knew that I had to get to the other side of the pool, and the only way to find success was to jump in.

A brand-new female insurance specialist here in the firm has just started out in sales. She struggles with negative self-talk and she doubts that she can accomplish what she has set out to do. I feel differently—otherwise, we would never have hired her! So I said to her, "You have to find out what motivates you. Is it a quote? Is it finding someone who inspires you? Is it music?"

I asked her some other questions as well, and these are good questions that you could ask yourself: "What gets you going in the morning? What lifts your spirit? What allows you to feel that you can accomplish anything?" **There's really no one else to pull ourselves out of this sense of self-doubt. It's an inside job that we have to do for ourselves.** I've pulled myself out of it, and I recognize it's a really big struggle for women to do the same thing. But you can. In this regard, your success will come from within.

Sometimes that sense of self-doubt evidences itself in terms of self-sabotaging behavior. When you don't believe you're capable, when you don't believe you have the skills or that you aren't smart enough, or that you aren't a dynamic speaker, or that you aren't engaging enough to get people to buy or take your advice, you tend to act on those beliefs as if they were true. So the question becomes this: How can we eliminate the negative talk that goes on subconsciously in our brains? When you do so, you can accomplish so much more. I remember when I first started out I would sit at my desk and tell myself, "I can't go see that client, because they're going to ask me a question and I don't have all the answers yet."

Well, guess what? I *still* don't have all the answers! I have figured out, however, a way to get in front of people and engage them, and build a relationship with them. As a result, I feel perfectly comfortable telling them I will get them the answers to the questions that I cannot answer on the spot. I had to get comfortable with the idea that I didn't know everything—and that I didn't *need* to know everything. If you allow all of these negatives to block you, you'll never go anywhere. So if you find yourself telling yourself, "I'm not capable, I'm not smart enough, I'm not engaging enough, I'm not an interesting person," realize you're not alone. These are thoughts that go through all women's minds—and probably some men's, too—as they begin a career in financial services. At least they did for me.

Another issue is that men are better at promoting themselves than women. I don't know why that's the case, and not all men are like this, but there's just something inside of a man, as far as I can tell, that always believes, "I've got this! I can do this!" At the same time, there's something inside of a woman that says, "I can't do that!"

Maybe it's something in our hormones. Maybe it's how our brains are wired. I just don't know. I can look at a man who's just starting out in this business and I'm sure that he has doubts and fears as well. But he's going to handle it differently from women. Maybe men are blessed to be born with a bigger ego than women! It certainly helps them in the business world, that's for sure. Whether it helps them in the rest of their lives, that's a question that's open to debate.

The reason I'm disclosing so much about my own fears and concerns is that as women read this book, I want them to say, "Hey, she wasn't anything special! She was a woman who started in this business with the same sort of doubts and fears I have, and look where she ended up. How the heck did she get there?"

The simple answer is that I didn't do anything earth-shattering. I just did my job. I dealt with the negative voices in my head. I overcame the obstacles I faced and I ended up in a pretty awesome place. I'm thrilled to be in that awesome place. I'm hoping that by sharing my own struggles, I can give hope to women who are new in the industry or who have been here for a while and are struggling. I want you to recognize that wherever you are, you can get through it and you can get to an amazing point, too.

Another issue is the question of what messages women receive when they're young—what do parents, teachers, older siblings, or mentor figures put in their heads at an early age that becomes part of the hardwiring? I'll start with my father. The message I always received from him was, "You need to work hard for whatever you get in life. You need to work hard to find success." That McNeely mentality became ingrained in me, because every McNeely works hard. I remember it vividly becoming part of my mindset from a very early age because I saw my father working hard to support my family. I saw my grandfather working hard, my uncles, my aunts, and anyone carrying the McNeely name—they were all driven to succeed. And that was the message I got from my father. Gender didn't matter because my parents had two daughters. There was no son, so he treated us like his legacy.

"Nothing will come easily to you," he would remind us. "You need to work hard to get what you want." As a result, it never crossed my mind that gender would be an obstacle for me. Never, ever. And I didn't know what I wanted to be when I grew up. I just knew that I was driven to succeed. So I was fortunate to grow up in a household where gender was never an obstacle.

I was also a team sports player. I played basketball, volley-ball, and softball, but basketball was my favorite sport. I also acted in plays. I was always in group activities. I remember from those days that girls were sometimes seen as second-rate when it came to sports. The boys' teams received most of the emphasis, and the girls' teams were just sort of nice to have around. Let's let them play basketball if they want to play basketball—that kind of thing. But it never reached the point that stunted my desire to succeed.

Looking back, those situations probably were a blessing because they allowed me to find out how to cope in those situations where I wasn't on the team of choice. I was in a second-best situation. But I didn't let that stop me from doing well or wanting to succeed.

When it came to my teachers, some were extremely moti-vational. They would say, "You can get anything you want. You can get whatever you want." There were others who took a different view and would tell us, "Remember, you're from a small town in Wisconsin. You're probably not going to go far." It depended on their own worldview, of course, whether they felt stuck in a small town, how big a world they saw for themselves. But I never allowed anything like that to change my mindset, that sense that I could accomplish anything.

So it was certainly not my circumstances that planted any seeds of doubt in my mind about my ability to succeed. Quite frankly, it just had to do with being a woman.

§

My parents divorced while I was growing up, and my mother did not work outside the home prior to the divorce. I remember being in awe of just how supportive she was as a parent. She played the traditional support role in our family, providing emotional support to my father, my sister, and me. She did it very, very well.

Later on, I developed an awareness of the motivation she gave me when she, herself, began in the financial services industry when her own world had been shattered by the divorce. She picked herself up and found herself a new career. She succeeded at that career despite the fact that it was a very difficult time for a woman to be in the insurance industry. So I felt incredibly inspired by her. As it happens, my mom was younger than I am now when she started, so sometimes I wonder, if I were to get divorced and have two children to support and had to start a whole new career, how motivated would I be to succeed? My mother used her situation to catapult her into the success that she's found. At the same time, she was always extremely inspirational to my sister and me, and to many other women as well.

I know that she had the same sort of self-doubt that I did. We've never spoken directly about it, but I can guarantee that that's the truth. I was a senior in high school when she started in financial services. At the time, it was just my mother and me living at home together, because my sister had gone away to college. I remember her coming home at 9 or 10 p.m., just spent by her long day of work. And she would often say, "I don't know if I can do this again tomorrow, but I'm going to." So I knew it was taxing, and I know she was trying to hold everything together, as women so often need to do. But I guarantee you she had a lot of negative self-talk going on.

§

Another key to overcoming fear and self-doubt is to find other people who inspire you. Now I'm talking about peers in the industry—these people can be your study group, other advisors, not necessarily just women, who have overcome obstacles and have gotten to a place of success. By any definition they *look* successful. Whether or not they *feel* successful is another conversation! But having people like that around you, supporting you, is a hugely important puzzle piece when it comes to getting rid of the negative self-talk. Instead, you find yourself saying, "If that person did it, I can do it too."

Remember, I cried every day when I started in this field. I remember thinking, "I've got to pull myself through this," and I did. It helps me to remember those moments as a point of reference so I can remind myself how far I've come. There can be positive lasting effects, as long as I don't allow them to be a continuation of the negative self-talk.

Even writing this book triggered more fear and self-doubt. I had to ask myself, do I really think I have anything to say that can help or inspire other people? It was difficult for me to commit to this at first, because I doubted that anyone would want to read what I have to say. It took me about a week to get my head around the idea of doing a book specifically about female advisors, and then I thought, this is the right move. This is the direction to take because other women will read this and say, "Oh my gosh, that's so me!"

I suppose that if I were a man, I might never have had any of those doubts. But then, I also might not be able to help the women I'm trying to reach with this book.

One of the benefits of confronting your own feelings is that it becomes much easier to be open and honest with others. The word "intimacy" can be understood as "into me, see." I also heard once that the definition of intimacy is being yourself with someone else. Right now, as I write, we are having our year-end planning meeting, and the meetings within my study group are very raw and very real. We have such incredible trust in one another. We've had sessions where we've cried the whole time, because someone poured out her heart to the rest of the group, or all of us poured out our hearts. I remember that our first in-person meeting was so raw because we were really getting to know each other and we wanted the space to be very safe. As a result, I can say that every one of the women in my study group is inspirational to me.

There are many reasons why the women are so inspi-rational, but it all comes down to the fact that they've overcome incredible obstacles. Because we're so open with each other, we've been able to see the good, the bad, and the ugly of everything we've gone through, whether it's divorce, having a child go through a difficult situation, not having the right mate in life, or not having the ability to have children because they haven't found that right mate, or even losing a loved one. These are things that we all may face. But when you have a group of people who make it safe for you to share, and you can trust yourself with them, you find enormous inspiration in that kind of setting. I know that if I allow myself to be real and raw and then pour everything out there, the group will help me pick things back up and guide me in the right direction.

Sometimes the support you need will come not from industry colleagues but from friends or family members. Earlier, I told the story about the day I sat in my father's office and poured out my heart to him, and he saw something in me, which helped him quell some of the negativity inside me. I call that moment the "goldmine" conversation. That conversation still motivates me to this day. You get those gold nuggets that provide you with ongoing motivation. It's important to deposit them somewhere where they're readily available in your brain. That way, when you're having a negative self-talk day, you can pull out that nugget and remind yourself, "There's a goldmine here. And I believe in you more than you believe in yourself right now."

Keep that nugget close, because some day you're going to need it. Every time you have that negative self-talk, you'll be able to draw on something positive to help you combat it. It will be there and it will be a constant thing.

Is it easier for women today in the workplace? No doubt. Just watch a *Mad Men* episode if you want to see what it was like for women not that many years ago. Because there are so many more women in the field, it's easier for Millennial agents than it is for Baby Boomers, just as it was easier for Boomers than it was for their parents' generation. And yet, Millennial women are going to have some of the same obstacles. I see many of them going through the same kind of struggles that women in my mother's generation and my generation (Gen X) went through. It definitely helps to have more female role models in the industry, but at the same time, women still go through those early years of self-doubt.

In some ways, the negativity never ends. I remember having a conversation with a friend of mine who had been appointed trustee at NAIFA a year before I was. I recall saying to him, "I don't think I've got anything to bring to the table."

He looked me in the eyes and he said, "Are you kidding me? You absolutely have something to bring to the table. You're going to figure that out really quickly when you sit down at that table."

He was right. He doesn't realize it, but that was exactly what I needed to hear at that moment. **So if the negative voices are always going to remain in our heads, it's essential to have other voices—those inside our own minds and those of supportive friends, in and out of the industry—to counter that negativity.** We always need to verify just how real those negative thoughts are. If we don't do that, we'll never get anywhere. We'll just keep listening to the negativity, and as a result, we won't live in reality. The best way to get a reality check is to run any negative thought you have by someone whom you know and trust. Tell on yourself! Let other people know the negative thoughts you're having. Don't be afraid of looking foolish or unusual. Everybody has those thoughts, if they're honest enough to admit it. The good news is that by telling on those thoughts, you'll take away their power and find your own.

Women are so much more powerful, effective, and capable than they give themselves credit for. So the time has come to stop listening to the negative voices in your head. They're not telling you the truth! We haven't met, but I know you're fabulous, and I know you can do anything. So just go out and do it!

VALUE ADDED:
FUNDS FOR THOUGHT

Try this exercise! It may take some discipline, but it will change your life. Diligently write down every negative thought you have in the course of a day, and if you can, every day for a week. As you're doing it, instantly come up with a positive thought about that topic. For example, if you have a staff meeting in an hour and are telling yourself the boss is going to come down on you for such-and-such, and that you deserve it, immediately chase that negative thought with one about a positive outcome—something that will remind you of your capabilities and empower you to handle that challenge and turn it around.

Chapter 8

Avoiding Misunderstandings in Business and Social Settings

AS WE'VE DISCUSSED, INSURANCE IS A GREAT AND often overlooked career for women. You can set your own hours, you can help people, and there is a huge shortfall of advisors in the industry. In other words, there are far more people out there who need good advice than are getting it! This includes the huge number of baby boomers entering retirement and a large number of Millennials, who either lack insurance, are under-insured, or don't even know what their insurance needs are.

Each year, insurance and financial services advisors in the United States leave the business due to either retirement or a phasing out of their careers. When you think about all the people who need help, and you think about the fact that it's inherent in women to want to help people, you can see how the industry can be a perfect fit.

I say "can be" because nothing's perfect, including our industry. Women leave our industry frequently, despite all the training we provide. If we are working hard to recruit women, we need to do a better job of holding onto them!

Part of the problem is that the men who run firms don't always take us seriously. *Mad Men* lives. Still. A man with old-school thinking might say (to himself, because he knows he'll get sued if he said it out loud), "Hey, I can't hire her, because if she has a kid, she'll be out for part of her pregnancy, and then there'll be maternity leave, or bedrest, or whatever. Or maybe I'll train her and then she'll decide not to come back to work." So we have to find ways to overcome that kind of thinking.

And then there's another issue that affects women much more directly, and that has to do with misunderstandings that can arise in business and social settings. So that's what we're going to talk about right now.

It's all too easy for a man to misinterpret the kind of interest a woman is showing in a business setting. I know that it's the 21st century, and the tendency may be to dismiss this kind of thing as totally 1950s or '60s, but denying it is risky. We all know that if we're going to get anywhere with a prospect, we have to be friendly, we have to be sociable, we have to display serious interest in the other person—all those good things. This is just as true for men as it is for women. With women, however, there's an added layer of complexity to every one of these conversations. Quite simply, men may take this kind of interest that we're displaying and misinterpret it. They may misinterpret it very, very badly!

This has to do with prospects or clients on the one hand, and other professionals in the industry, because if we're going to succeed we have to spend time connecting with others in our field. Much of the work that higher-level insurance advisors receive comes when they are splitting complex cases with other advisors. So we'll come back to the question of dealing with people in the industry and start first with clients.

I had a situation early on in my career where I needed to connect with a young man who needed to enroll in a retirement plan. So I had to set up a time with him to have a conversation about that. As we spoke, for some reason, I had this sense that I needed to be a little bit careful. The main thing is always to trust your instincts. So the first thing I did was to make sure that we would meet in a public place. Since the meeting consisted of just him and me, I asked him to meet me at a restaurant. As a woman, I did not feel comfortable going to his home. It's important for women to be aware of our surroundings and the places where we are meeting our prospects and clients. If you've never met someone, is it really such a great idea to go to his house or apartment for a first meeting? Or for any meeting?

Public places are so much better for the kinds of conversations we need to have. If we are meeting in an elegant hotel lobby, or a nice restaurant, we are conveying an image of class. A friend of mine once said, "A cup of coffee costs just as much at a Starbucks as at a Ritz-Carlton, so why not go to the Ritz-Carlton?" Okay, in reality, that cup of coffee at the Ritz-Carlton costs a little more, but it certainly adds a touch of class to a meeting to conduct in the lobby of a fine hotel! Whether you prefer hotel lobbies, restaurants, or any other public place is perfectly fine with me. The key is that you are choosing a place where the message you're sending is that the conversation you're going to have is strictly business.

The meeting I had with that individual went fine, but I think the setting I chose had a lot to do with the meeting's success. **Women have to be aware of their surroundings.** Is it unfair that a man has more freedom and can meet a client or prospect at home, sitting at the kitchen table, where the prospect or client is most comfortable? Of course it is! But nobody ever said the world was going to be fair.

We must also trust our instincts. If you sense that there might be trouble, then it would be absurd to propose a location for a meeting—your place or his—that could bring on trouble. **It's also a very good idea to let others know where you are. It's not a good thing if you're out there meeting and talking with people and no one knows your schedule.** Bad things happen in the world. Recently, there was a story about a realtor in the Midwest who went out to do a showing for a house and was murdered. Obviously this is an extreme example, but these are the times in which we live. You must protect yourself. Any female professional needs to be vigilant. Sometimes vigilance means bringing someone else along to the meeting so that you're not there alone. It never hurts to have someone else there, whether it's a man or a woman, by your side. In my career, there have been a few occurrences when I was uncomfortable, and I did what I needed to do to reduce the discomfort—and reduce the risk.

Bottom line: meet in a public place. Bring someone with you if you can. And make sure someone else knows your schedule.

The next point: know your boundaries. There is no bit of business that is worth putting yourself in a risky situation in order to obtain it. If you feel as though a line has been crossed, exit the situation right then and there. Let the sale go. Let the connection go. There is nothing worth that risk.

These days, most of my client appointments take place in my office. When I started, most of my meetings took place in the households of my prospects and clients. After a while, I shifted to public places and my office. Doing so has raised my comfort level drastically. The time when you meet someone is also something to which you should pay attention. My staff knows not to schedule anything for me after hours. It's not that there's a concern about violence, although these are crazy times. It's simply about avoiding uncomfortable situations. If we're giving off inappropriate signals, bad things can happen. My entire office is very responsive and alert to all of the signs that would potentially concern us—a prospect or client wanting to meet at an unusual hour, or if there's something else about the meeting that raises a red flag. We've been given instincts for a reason. **So often, when we override our instincts, especially in pursuit of a sale, we open ourselves up to trouble.**

In all of these matters, don't distinguish between people who are married or single. Married men can cause plenty of trouble, too! I've had awkward situations with both single men and married men in my career. Not often, but it has happened. Early in my career, I met a prospect in a restaurant. So we were in a safe place. He was married, and I still felt extremely uncomfortable because of the way he was talking. He actually became a client, but not for long. He ended up ignoring all of my advice. I quite frankly wondered if his motives in working with me had nothing to do with saving money. Eventually, his account phased out, and he closed it, and that was that. But it was certainly an awkward situation at the time. You've really got to ask yourself whether a fee that a potentially troublesome client might generate will be worth the headaches, fear, and potential risks.

§

So far, we've been talking about situations where we are meeting clients one on one. Let's turn now to the question of receptions, cocktail parties, conventions, seminars, or other settings where we meet, network, and socialize with many new people. In these settings, the rules are the same. Know your surroundings. Know your settings. And know your limits. You can be friendly and yet still have boundaries. It once happened at an industry meeting that a man I met made some inappropriate comments in the middle of a very interesting networking conversation. As soon as he made those comments, I said, "This conversation is over," and I walked away. We were in a public setting—it wasn't like the two of us were alone somewhere. He made his inappropriate comments in a room filled with people. But I ended the conversation at that moment and set that boundary very clearly. To this day, whenever I see him at industry events, I ignore him, because I have set that boundary. He crossed a line. **As far as I'm concerned, there are certain lines that are non-negotiable. I highly recommend that you set your own non-negotiable lines as well.**

It's very painful, as a professional, to acknowledge that this kind of thing still goes on. But the reality is that women face these kinds of awkward moments when they are in professional settings. This is especially true when they're alone—a line can be crossed. It's up to us to be astute enough to control the situation. If you're seen as a very strong professional woman, you are less likely to find yourself out of control or in a situation you cannot handle. The minute that you flounder or waver on your boundaries, all of a sudden you're no longer seen as strong or professional. In a sense, you are fair game for whatever a man wants to say.

Keep in mind that what you allow others to do to you, and how you allow others to speak to you, ultimately determines how they view you. If a man is strong, he's admired for that fact. If a woman is strong, people say she's a bitch. The reality is that you don't have to be a mean person to be a strong, entrepreneurial woman. But you must have clear boundaries and very clear lines that you will not allow others to cross in professional settings.

To reiterate, it's best to take another advisor with you if you are going to meet someone outside the office. If you feel a bit uncertain about a prospect, you can tell him (or her), "I'm only taking appointments in my office." They don't need to know that you see other clients in their homes. If you feel that a line might potentially be crossed, then you control the situation by controlling where you meet, who's there with you, and when you meet.

You don't necessarily have to bring another agent with you. Even if it's a person on your administrative staff, that's smart.

Ultimately, what we do every day can be defined as relationship-building. Sometimes, when you're trying to build a professional relationship, it can be misconstrued as if you're trying to build a personal relationship. I've always been clear with my clients. Sometimes I have single male clients, and I always make clear to them, if the subject arises, of course, that I don't date my clients. Sometimes a man will say, "Hey, would you like to go for coffee?" I explain in a friendly way that I make it a practice not to date clients. Typically, they're okay with that and they'll say something like, "Well, that makes sense." If you make it clear that this is a general principle of yours, you won't be insulting the person. Too often, women are afraid of hurting someone's feelings, and they put themselves in uncomfortable or even dangerous situations. They cannot afford to do that in today's world.

The good news is that things are much better than they were. A woman friend of mine, a mentor figure in my life, started in the industry about thirty years ago. She worked in a male-dominated agency setting, and it was just brutal. She would tell me stories about how isolated and alone she felt, how misunderstood she was, and how the men either communicated poorly with her or spoke extremely inappropriately.

Today, we have laws about some of these things, but those laws are often broken. I have such respect for this individual because she lived through a very difficult era and survived, and remains in the industry, where she is considered a powerhouse today. The obstacles she had to overcome regarding the one issue of treatment from her male colleagues astounded me. Sometimes it was simple as a man saying, "You're a woman. You're never going to amount to what the male advisors are in this office." Or they would give her a crummy desk or a lesser space because they said she didn't deserve a nicer office. This is how it was years ago, in what you can call the *Mad Men* era in insurance. We've come so far. The industry is still male-dominated, but it is accepting women as equals to a much greater degree than ever before. It's definitely shifting. The fact that I was elected president of an organization that went 125 years without a female president signifies something.

It's funny—although maybe funny isn't the right word. Even in my role as NAIFA president, there were still inappropriate moments. The story that I told earlier about an individual making inappropriate comments and I told him the conversation was over—that occurred while I was in my role as president of NAIFA. Others have come up to me, referenced my gender, and questioned my ability to handle my role. Let's face it. **Words matter. How you treat people matters.** A comment along the lines of "I didn't even think you were capable of being NAIFA president"—I just never expected to hear something like that after reaching that position. But the reality is that some people think it, and others voice it. If we all could take a step back and think before we speak, maybe we would scare away many fewer women. So it's not surprising that two out of five women walk away from the industry before they've made it. It's hard enough to sell insurance. It's hard enough to knock on doors, cold call, and enter into the sorts of conversations that most people would rather never have.

People don't want to think about loss, injury, or death. They just want to go about their lives and hope that nothing bad happens. They certainly don't want to spend money on insurance when they could spend it on something else or just keep it in the bank. When you add on this additional layer, it certainly complicates things. Men may have it easier, but life isn't perfect for them, either. People can be pretty atrocious to male insurance advisors, not just women! Is it harder for women? I have no doubt. Can we do it? Of course we can.

Sometimes the shift from professional to personal can happen so quickly that you barely pick up on it. When we're chitchatting and trying to get to know people, the key is always to tie things back to the professional part of the conversation. As in "Hey, you told me that you were hoping to retire by age fifty-five. That is so cool. You know,

I think we can help you figure that out. I get really excited by people who really have the drive to achieve a goal quicker than most others. Tell me a little bit more about what retirement looks like for you."

You don't have to use those exact words, of course. But whatever you're talking about, always tie it back to the professional side when you're having a conversation with a client.

If you're attending something in a social setting, industry meeting, conference, or any public gathering, this shouldn't even have to be said, but I'm going to say it anyway: don't drink too much. Or don't even drink at all. I've often seen people get themselves into situations they could have avoided had they not been drinking. If you drink too much in public, you may no longer be capable of drawing a line—of setting boundaries. You just cannot let yourself go beyond the point of no control. Typically, alcohol can make that happen without the drinker even realizing it. Again, I've seen it so often and I found myself thinking, "Oh, my gosh! That woman went beyond where she should've gone, and now her line is gone. She doesn't even know the line exists anymore."

Drinking too much changes people's perception of you, and you just don't want that to happen. Even if the worst thing that happened was that people saw you in a different light, and nothing inappropriate or dangerous happened, isn't that bad enough?

In conversations with prospects, I like to think that I'm good at asking questions, but I am also deliberate with the words I choose. The goal is to be careful enough with your words so that you are not leading people in a direction that you did not intend. You want to avoid anything that could be mistaken as a double entendre, as a hint or signal that your interest in the person you're speaking with goes beyond the professional. If you're deliberate about the words you choose, that's far less likely to happen.

Again, men also have to be careful about this kind of thing. I know men who have been put in difficult situations where they're out with a group of clients, and the clients wanted to go to a strip club. So men have to draw their own lines in the sand as well. Again, never put yourself in a situation where you are uncomfortable. No sale is worth that.

My only concern about the advice in this chapter is that you're going to think, Juli, why would I want to open myself up to all these potentially risky or even dangerous situations? The good news is that such inappropriate moments have been few and far between over the course of my career. I attribute that fact to the guidance I've offered in this chapter. **Meet people in public places, not their homes. Bring someone along, if possible. Have boundaries, and adhere to those boundaries. Never let dollar signs override your instincts about people. Don't let alcohol loosen your tongue or your boundaries in social settings—there's really no**

reason to drink on the job. Make sure that someone on your team knows your schedule, so that if you aren't checking in or calling back after a meeting, people will know where you are and who you were meeting.

If we were talking about the *Mad Men* era, perhaps I might caution you against a career in insurance. Fortunately, the world has evolved, at least to some degree, since the era we saw depicted on that TV show. If you're professional, smart, and follow these simple guidelines to keep yourself safe, you'll have nothing to worry about. **Just remember that you dictate the way other people will perceive you.** If your boundaries are clear from the beginning, if you choose your words carefully, and if you cut off any situations the moment they start to go south, you'll have nothing to worry about. All will be well. I find it extremely enjoyable to have working friendships with my clients. Getting to know them, and helping to meet their professional and financial needs, is extremely satisfying—not to mention, it may be lucrative. If you know how to handle yourself, you'll be great.

VALUE ADDED: FUNDS FOR THOUGHT

How do you want people to see you? What are some of the qualities you bring to the table that can inspire others?

Chapter 9

Insurance Is No Longer a Hard Sell: It's Taught and Bought

WHEN MY FATHER STARTED IN THE BUSINESS MORE than forty years ago, life insurance was seen as a hard sell. As we've discussed, people just trusted him. He beat the streets. He went out there. He was constantly talking about life insurance. He was selling it. He was educating in a way, but it wasn't the same sort of education as takes place today.

That's because the old school was hard sell, and the new school—the way we operate today—is really more that you're educated, and then you buy. That's what we're going to talk about in this chapter: how the selling of insurance has changed, and why the new model is so much more beneficial to women as agents and advisors.

A lot of the time, when a woman thinks about selling insurance, she thinks about some slick, loudmouthed guy in a bad suit pulling a fast one on some unsuspecting prospects, shoving a pen into their hands to get a signature, and then running out the door. Whether there was any truth to that model in the past, I'll leave to others to decide. I will say that that outmoded stereotype has nothing to do with the way we sell insurance today. And again, that's good news for women. In this chapter, I'll explain exactly why.

There's so much more information available to consumers today. Prior to any meeting I have with a client now, I expect that they will have done a lot of research. They'll go out and read articles and try to understand what they're purchasing. In the past, in my father's world, everything was based on a trust factor. You just trusted your agent that he was steering you toward a product you needed.

It's not that customers don't trust advisors today; it's just that so much information is available, so why not check it out and educate yourself?

Today, people won't just take your word for it. They're going to check their sources, and they have a lot of sources they can examine. So those advisors who do a really good job of educating and getting to the emotional side of the sale today do much better than those who still think the hard sell is the way to go. And when it comes to educating and getting to the emotional side of things, women have a serious advantage.

Today, we also find the rise of the robo-advisor. I recently saw a statistic that eight out of ten insurance decisions are now made online, and people are buying their insurance products online.[1] Some people even wonder whether there will still be a need for a human being to sell financial services, or whether everything will just go to robo-advisors and a do-it-yourself approach. The simple answer is that everyone's situation is unique. When you have a cookie-cutter approach, you run the risk of missing a significant factor in the decision-making process. When you have a human being, it's personalized, and therefore the recommendations that come back are also personalized. And again, this is where women shine—in getting to know not just the facts but the feelings, and often the facts that people may not be open to revealing at the very first moment.

For example, let's say we think about a young family, with the parents in their early thirties, two young kids, a dog, and a mortgage. But you shouldn't make assumptions! Maybe one of the spouses has some health issues, and we need to make sure we can get coverage before things get worse. Or maybe there's a family history of health issues, and we want to get as much coverage as possible before that

---

[1] LIFE and LIMRA 2011 Insurance Study, www.limra.com, accessed February 2016; PwC Analysis.

person runs the risk of succumbing to those same health issues. A robo-advisor isn't going to be able to recognize those sorts of things, because most people would never disclose that sort of information to a website. A cookie-cutter approach just doesn't cut it. That's why the human touch is so important.

Another problem is that people could just pull a few articles off the Internet, find themselves pointed in one direction about their insurance solutions, and then they think that's the only option they have. They may not have the knowledge base or even the desire to dive deeply enough to find out that they have three other options. That's why having a human advisor is such a critical thing. It's the same thing as making assumptions about your health care. Would you ever go online and read something and then decide that you needed surgery, just based on an article you read on the Internet? Your financial health is just as important as your physical health. So why would you put your financial health at risk when you don't have to?

Today, if you're going to overcome the allure of the robo-advisor, you have to be good at building relationships. For men or women, that's the way we distribute financial services in this day and age. We're taking an educational approach. Personally, I've never been comfortable with the hard sell. The "taught and bought" approach has been the only way I've been comfortable working throughout my entire career. So if we're going to talk about creating a relationship with a client, then we need to discuss the emotional side of selling.

Women have a very good way of picking up on emotions, and they also have very clear ways of conveying emotions. **This serves us well in our profession because so much of insurance on the risk side—life insurance, disability insurance, and long-term care insurance, for example— is very much based on emotion.** If we can educate our clients and then pull in the emotional component, we have a great chance of finding success. Women have a really great skillset in this area. It's not to say that men can't do it, because I think they can, but women absolutely have the skills to sell emotionally charged products.

Women by nature are very nurturing. They're great communicators. They tend to use more words than men. **And when you think about it, money is a very emotional subject.** No matter what gender you are, money really pushes people's buttons. You want to make money. You want to hold on to it. You want to invest it properly. You don't want it to go away. **Money is not devoid of emotion: it's a hot topic and also an intimate topic.** Marriages are made and broken over financial issues. So when clients or prospects sit at their kitchen table and open up their checkbooks and reveal their financial situations, they are really pouring their hearts out to us. How we handle that openness becomes critical. It's such an important part for us building that relationship with the client.

It just takes me back to the days watching my father early on in my career. Of course, he had great relationships with his clients. He would say, "This is what you need. Here's the application. Sign here." And I would look at him, feeling just mortified, and I would say, "I can't do that with my clients!"

First, if I didn't have a relationship with the person, how could I ask the prospect or client to trust me and sign something? Second, I'm just a young punk kid whom they probably don't even trust. What would make them sign something if they didn't understand it?

So immediately in my mind, I realized I needed to focus on making sure my clients fully understood what they were buying before they just signed on the dotted line. The approach my father taught me was very foreign to me. I transitioned to becoming very much a teacher. **I actually say to clients, "My job is to make sure you understand what you have. If I don't explain it in a way that you fully understand, I want you to interrupt me, and I want you to ask me to explain it again in a different way. And so, don't feel bad, because if I can't explain it to you, then I have no expectation of you being willing to buy it."** Frequently, clients will say, "I appreciate that."

And by being open in this manner, it would create the give-and-take kind of dialogue I wanted to have with my prospects, because they truly wanted to understand what they were buying.

The younger clientele I was working with twenty years ago was just like me. They wanted to truly understand a purchase before they made it. Men and women are the same way: they both have to feel comfortable asking questions. I would say things like, "There's no such thing as a stupid question." And they would say, "Well, then, in that case, I have a silly question!" I would reply, "There's no silly question! I probably have a silly answer, if you think it's that silly a question!"

The key is to make people feel very comfortable, because everyone can have roadblocks. As I said, when you're talking about your finances, it's personal. **If your prospects and clients aren't comfortable asking you serious questions, they'll never be truly comfortable with you as their advisor.** As a result, much of what I focused on early in my career was to make sure that everyone felt comfortable. I would even say things like, "I may not have all the answers, but I can promise you that I'm going to get you the answer that you need clarified, because that's what this is all about. You need to be completely comfortable with what you're getting into, and if you don't understand it, we're going to make sure we continue to work through it."

§

Here's another piece of guidance for women in the industry. Often, in a marriage you'll have one spouse who handles the finances and the other wants nothing to do with it. They don't even want to come to the meeting. They want to let the other person handle things, as I talked about in

Chapter 2. I am insistent upon the couple coming together, because if they don't, there's a chance that the person who isn't there won't fully understand what I'm recommending. I'll say, "I understand that this isn't their forte, and this isn't what they like to do. But if I don't have them here, I have no chance of making sure they understand. And they truly do need to have at least a small understanding of what you're investing in or what you're purchasing, because if they don't, I have not done my job."

It's such a change from the days when women were just completely excluded. It wouldn't even be a thought in the mind of the (male) advisor or the client, for that matter! Neither would think twice about it. This kind of situation is absolutely foreign to Gen X and Millennials. It would never even occur to them to exclude a spouse from an important meeting with an advisor. It just wouldn't go there.

This is why it's essential, if we're going to set ourselves apart as advisors and overcome the robo-advisor phenomenon, to focus on personalized service. We have to provide personalized conversations and personalized advice, because people can get generic advice anywhere. The buying habits of the American consumer have changed. Your bedside manner, as the doctors used to say, is just as important as your product knowledge. But we were typically never taught any of that. Today, medical schools are giving more and more attention to the relationship between the doctor and the patient. We need to follow the lead of our doctor friends and do exactly that—focus on the relationship and not just on the results we're trying to create.

The industry has also grown in terms of understanding the psychology of sales and the dynamic of working with a couple. The first designation I ever received was LUTCF, which stands for Life Underwriter Training Council Fellow. It was sales skills. The training focused somewhat on product, but mostly it had to do with the sales process and sales skills. The designation also included some of the psychology of sales. It was one of the best designations I've ever had and it definitely set me up to build my own destiny and create a process of dealing with people in my own practice, so that was definitely invaluable. But did it go far enough? Does a focus on sales skills really address today's consumer mindset? Obviously not. I received that designation about eighteen years ago, so it's been a long time! We advisors have to stay up to date with how consumers want to be taught. Today, I would assume that most companies have some sort of psychology of sales training, but I don't know how important they consider it to be.

A highly renowned leader in the financial services industry, Susan Cooper, CLU, ChFC, CFP, CDFA, CAP, president and CEO of Empire Wealth Strategies—Penn Mutual's career agency in New York City—authored a paper titled "What Women Need to Be Successful in the

Financial Services Industry With a Special Focus on Millennial Women." In that study, Cooper states that the "#1 aspect important to young top performers" surveyed in studies she cites was "helping people."[2] To that end, companies should know that focusing on sales skills and strategies that teach, rather than preach, is within the realm of helping prospects and clients choose solutions that they understand and that they subsequently feel confident and comfortable buying.

So much of what I do on a day-to-day basis is just simply helping individuals, couples, and families. I'm a sounding board. I listen to concerns and problems, and then I navigate a plan as to how we can help overcome the problems they face.

§

When it comes to really listening, who do you think has the biggest advantage, men or women? You'd better believe it's women! This is truly a service profession. There's no denying that. **You're serving others well so that they can live well. If you take care of people, your business will thrive. It's got to be all about them, not about you. There's a certain amount of sublimation of ego here, and again, this plays to the strengths of women.**

It also helps you get referrals. People will often say, "Oh, you need to talk to Juli! I leave her office feeling completely

---

[2] What Do Women Need to be Successful in the Financial Services Industry. Susan Cooper, CLU (R) CEO, Empire Wealth Strategies.

in control. Juli and her team don't just talk at you, they talk to you and educate you on what you need to know to make an educated decision."

That's the kind of referral you want to aim for—not just, "She really knows the ins and outs of long-term care insurance." If you have a client who says all of this to a friend of hers, then you've got another client coming your way. That's the kind of powerful endorsement you're looking for. When women think about going into a helping profession, they most likely think about teaching or nursing. These are great professions, and they serve the world so beautifully. But don't leave out being a financial advisor! It's not just about closing cases and making money. It's really about helping people. The word "service" is built right into financial services. So I wish more women would recognize that they can serve people in this manner. Not everybody is cut out to be a teacher or a nurse. And we in financial services do have that negative image to overcome—that sense that we are just snake oil salespeople, used car salespeople, whatever you want to say. I wish the industry did a better job of overcoming these negative images, because in reality, we're here to help. We may not even be compensated right away for the help we're providing, but it invariably does come around.

They called my father's generation the "silent generation." They were silent because they took what life gave them and didn't question it. That's no longer how the world works:

everybody questions everything. So if you really want to succeed in this world—and you can—recognize that you bring incredible strength to the table just the way you are.

VALUE ADDED:
FUNDS FOR THOUGHT

In your own life, how likely are you to purchase something you know little or nothing about for yourself and your family, just because somebody said you should?

Chapter 10

How Defining Moments Can Show
You How Far You've Come

WHEN I WAS NEW TO THE INDUSTRY, I WORKED
with a couple in their late thirties, a farm family with three
children. My client had an old insurance policy that was
no longer meeting his needs. He called and said, "I need to
meet with you and talk about this." I was happy, because
I had been trying to get him to come in for a while. He
came to my office, but he came alone—he didn't bring his
wife. We sat and talked and finally he said, "I don't know
what I can do. I know I don't have enough money to keep
that policy going."

We ended up writing him a ten-year term policy for one
hundred thousand dollars. That's all he said he could afford

at the time. He went through the underwriting process, he was accepted, and the company put the policy in force.

The reason I tell you this story is because three years later, I got a phone call from his wife. She was crying.

"I don't remember if we still have that life insurance policy with your firm," she sobbed, "but my husband died of a massive heart attack this morning. And I need to know if we still have a policy."

Naturally, I immediately remembered him.

"Yes, he has a policy. I don't want you to worry about anything. I will get everything together. I'd like to come and sit down with you next week."

We made an appointment. I went to her house and we sat at her kitchen table. We were both crying, because she had just lost her husband. He had been milking the cows and just keeled over in the barn from that heart attack. At that point, he was in his early forties. Their oldest son was seventeen and he vowed to help his mom help the farm, and he said he was going to do everything he could and still go to school.

She's telling me all this as I'm filling out the paperwork so that I can deliver her a check for one hundred thousand dollars. She's crying, of course, and I'm crying, too, because I immediately felt the gravity of the situation. I also realized that I wished I had pushed him harder to write a bigger policy, because they owed more than one hundred thousand dollars in various debts.

I will never forget that moment. Now, when a client comes in and says, "I can only afford this much," I push a whole lot harder. I tell the client, "You need this much. Let's figure out how to get you what you need versus what you think you can afford."

I am much more driven in those situations because of that moment. I'm not trying to sell more so I can just make a bigger commission. I'm trying to help meet the needs of my clients, even when they would rather not spend money on an insurance policy. I'll never forget that moment with that farm wife. I vividly remember sitting at the table, and my heart was breaking, because I didn't feel I had done my job. And yet, that one hundred thousand dollars meant the world to her, because it was way more than she thought they had. They were able to keep the farm for a period of time. They ultimately sold it, but this is what we do. **This is the *purpose* of what we do. We help families continue to maintain their lifestyle at a time when all hell has broken loose in their lives. We try to put some financial stability in place when they have no stability anywhere else.**

I'm telling you this story not only because I want you to keep this in mind the next time you're working with a client who tells you that he or she cannot afford the policy that is truly needed. Of course I want you to push back hard. But I'm telling you this for another reason. In my career, that situation at the kitchen table in that farm house was what I would call a defining moment. **Defining moments are those situations that you can use not just to learn from and become a better agent, as important as that is. In addition, I want you to use those defining moments to show yourself just how far you've come. And that's what I want to discuss with you in this chapter.**

Defining moments, from my perspective, are pivotal moments in life, either personal or professional, when suddenly you make a shift, you hit a high, or you even hit a low point. **These defining moments are the times that contribute vitally to the person you are and the person you are becoming.** So I'd like you to reflect on your own life and ask yourself, what are the defining moments that have made you who you are?

I'll give you some examples from my own life and career so that you have some guideposts as you think about your own life. Of course, for me, the classic defining moment was the day I had that conversation with my father in his office when he said to me, "There's a goldmine here." At that moment, I realized, he's right. And I realized that he saw something in me that I didn't see in myself, and it was time for me to go out and find it and get it and make my own success. For me, that was a defining moment.

Sometimes a defining moment is a situation that matters enormously to you, although it may not seem like the biggest deal to people around you. I remember when I got my CFP (CERTIFIED FINANCIAL PLANNER™) designation. I had been working on that for a number of years. When I finally passed that test, I remember thinking, "This is huge." At the time, it was defining me in terms of who I was going to be as an advisor. So that's an example of a professional defining moment—it's when you accomplish something that causes you to see yourself in a different light.

Another professional defining moment was when I made MDRT—Million Dollar Round Table—for the first time. Back then, I probably had to make about seventy-five thousand dollars in first-year commissions. That was the first time I qualified. The number goes up every year. At this point, the figure is closer to ninety thousand dollars in first-year commissions. Again, that was a defining moment, because now I had concrete evidence that my industry considered me to be among the best of the best. You just see yourself differently when other people see you in a certain way.

I mentioned that some defining moments are not the happy occasions of life. When I was taking care of my mother when she had cancer for the third time, that shifted my definition of success, and it shifted my definition of who I am. Often, we think of success as solely financial, or in terms of our employment status. And yet, success for me, after my mom was diagnosed, was all about how much time I could have with her. So if my job permitted me to have some of those precious moments with her, I was successful that day. The experience shifted my brain in terms of what's important.

That's why I've always said that your definition of success changes. It's not always going to be etched in stone. For example, I once asked an advisor, "What's your definition of success?" She had been in the business a long time.

"Success," she replied, "to me, is spending time with my grandkids." That was all that mattered to her at that point. She had a great career. She was paying the bills and then some. She was producing at a nice, high level. But that didn't matter nearly as much as being with her grandchildren. At that point in her life, that was success. That's why it's important to know that the definition of success that each of us will have is bound to change from year to year, sometimes from month to month, and sometimes even from day to day. **That's because you can have a defining moment—like the moment I learned about my mother's cancer—that completely changes the way you look at life.** I can tell you that the financial goal I had set for myself that year no longer mattered. I still wanted to strive to get there, but what mattered—and what success meant to me—was having a job that would allow me to be with my mom.

In addition to defining moments, I also have a category of events I call bursting moments. These are the really exciting times and moments where you say to yourself, "Oh, my gosh. I have found success!"

When I was elected NAIFA secretary, that was a bursting moment for me. "How in the world did I get here?" I asked myself. The feeling inside was such that I thought I just wanted to burst. That's why I call it a bursting moment! And what happens is that when you experience that kind of moment, you want to create it again and again. You want to have more amazing successes that make you say, "I've made it! I've gotten to where I wanted to be!" So that's really the difference between defining moments and bursting moments. **A defining moment is a situation, positive or negative, that radically changes the way you look at your life and the world. Bursting moments are those times when you cannot even control the happiness and joy and sense of accomplishment you're feeling because you made it. You got there. But then immediately, you want to find another bursting moment!**

Let's return to the subject of defining moments. What's remarkable about them is that they're subconscious events; you may not even realize at the time that you've been through one. It's only upon self-reflection later when you realize, "That was a real shift. That's when I changed. That's when I internalized a new understanding about myself and I realized I had to do something different in order to find success."

When I speak at events and I discuss the concept of defining moments, I think about the five Rs related to them: remember, responsibility, respect, reflect, and reset.

First, when I've had a defining moment, I try to **remember** that moment. How can I get this ingrained in my brain, so that I can go back and remember it? For example, a conversation with my father at the round table in his office is ingrained in my brain. I will never forget the "there's a goldmine here" conversation. I wanted to remember that shift I made that day, because it was monumental for me.

Responsibility is the next step. It was at that moment when I realized that it was my responsibility for me to find my own success. My dad was not going to make me successful. Neither was my mom. Neither would the company with which I had affiliated myself. *I* was going to make myself successful, and I had to take responsibility for that. That's when interior shift happened. That's what helped me move forward from that defining moment.

The third R is **respect.** We have to respect the lessons we have learned. Sometimes they're painful. Sometimes you ask yourself, "Why is this happening to me? Why is it happening now?" There's a reason. I truly believe everything happens for a reason. It may be difficult to respect that learning moment when it happens, but we can look back and respect it.

And then it's up to us to **reflect** on it often. If you have truly stored it in your memory, it will be easy for you to reflect back on that moment later on. It's really important to show yourself how far you've come.

And the final R, which is a critical piece in our ongoing growth, is to **reset.** If this truly was a defining moment and it caused me to shift significantly, I now needed to reset my definition of success. Again, going back to the goldmine conversation, my definition of success prior to that moment was really low. As in "I'm going to get up and I'm going to try to do this job." Success equaled making a sale. After that conversation, my definition of success changed. My self-talk went this way: "This is my career. I love what I do, and I'm going to go after it. Not only will I make a sale, but I'm going to make my goal this year." So you reset your definition based on those defining moments.

I recommend going through this process every time you have a defining moment. Frankly, I would be surprised if most people didn't have defining moments at least once or twice a year, and maybe more than that. It's a really good time at year's end to reflect on your year and look back for the defining moments. I'm certain there will be a couple of events throughout the past twelve months during which you already shifted and reset your goals. You don't have to write any of these things down. You can if you want to, if it helps you to internalize things. But I don't. I typically try to find a quiet place. Often, this might be in bed, in the shower, or just curled up on my couch with a fuzzy blanket. I really try to reflect back on that moment and go through this five-step process, allowing it to expand me from the inside and reset my definition of success.

I'm making a distinction here between goal setting and the kind of success mindset that I'm talking about right now. **Goals, from my perspective, are just benchmarks.** They're steps along the way to get you to success, but you're not successful just because you hit your goals. Goals are objectives or can reflect something that you're trying to get. **Success is when you know you've "gotten there."** I do write my goals down. I have a business plan on an annual basis. I know exactly what I want to do with regard to my professional and personal goals for the year. I write all of that down, because those need to be looked at throughout the year. I do have to have goals on a daily basis—something I'm shooting for. But ultimately, what matters is the success piece, what I advise people to experience when they go through those five Rs.

When you do reach the new level of success, it's important not to let your ego run away with you. You do have to take responsibility for your success, but don't let it go to your head! That's why I say respect the work that you've done to reach that point, but don't be egotistical about it. By the same token, when some people reach a sense of success, they start to ask themselves, "Okay, look where I am. I reached that goal. Maybe I can just coast for a while."

I don't believe in coasting. After all, when you think about a car, it can only coast one way—downhill! Success doesn't mean reaching a level that you wanted to reach and then stopping. It means continuing to grow, continually asking what's next, where are we going, how are we going to get there, and how are we going to push ourselves harder as a team? Sometimes the people around me get frustrated with me because they think I'm never satisfied. But I have no intention of being stagnant, and neither should you.

As we've discussed, there's so much negativity in the world, and we women internalize more than our fair share. Women constantly deal with that negativity. **That's why if we can replace the negativity with not just the defining moments but also those bursting moments—the moments where we burst with success—we'll have a much easier time dealing with the difficult things in life.** It's also good for us to remember those moments on a regular basis, because that helps us silence those negative voices. Anything we can do to silence that negativity is important. If you have a lot of things in your arsenal to counteract the negativity, you'll be prepared when something crazy or negative happens. You'll say, "Yeah, okay, this happened, but I'm not a failure. I might have missed on this one, but I also did this, this, and this, and I remember how good that felt. And I'm going to get there again!" That's the sort of mental thing I do. Maybe I'm crazy, but it works!

So when we talk about success, what exactly do we mean? For most people, success comes in three categories: our purpose, our health, and our relationships.

The financial services industry offers people very purpose-filled occupations. There are very few jobs or careers where you can be so fulfilled by doing what you do every day. The story with which I began this chapter, about the farmer's family—well, that's a perfect illustration for me of living my purpose. What a privilege it was to be able to serve that family by making sure that they had a policy in place, even if it wasn't what it could have been. If I hadn't acted, he might well have allowed his prior policy to lapse, and then he would have been totally uninsured when he unexpectedly passed away. So that's an example of how I get to live my purpose by working in this field.

Next, when it comes to health, we have both defining moments and bursting moments, too. We don't realize how important our health is until it's gone. Let me tell you a story about my cousin Paul. He took over the property/casualty, or home and auto, business from his father. There was always a plan that he would take over his dad's business and I would take over my dad's business. We have become really close over the years, and we would joke all the time about how we would do great things with our businesses once we got rid of the old guys!

So one day I was sitting in my office and my grandmother came in, and she was frantic.

"Juli, I need your help."

"What's going on, Grandma?" I asked, concerned.

"Well, I went past the Loyal office—" We had two offices, one in Spencer, and one in Loyal, about ten miles apart. "And the ambulance was out front. I didn't think anything of it until the ambulance went by on the road to Spencer with the lights on and the sirens blaring. I've got to find out what happened."

I made a few phone calls and found out that Paul was in the ambulance. They were rushing him to the hospital. They got him to the ER, because they thought he was having a heart attack. Paul was just twenty-nine years old.

We went to the ER, where they told us that the emergency room doctor had recognized that this was not a heart attack. They believed that Paul was suffering from something called a dissected aorta, which was typically not survivable. So the ER doctor had brought in the cardiologist on call, and thankfully he was an expert in the area of dissected aortas.

He told Paul, "We need to get you into surgery immediately, or you're going to die."

So they rushed him into surgery. They were able to stop the bleeding. They were in surgery for eight hours.

When they were done, they said, "Well, we've stopped the bleeding, but he's not out of the woods. The next twenty-four to forty-eight hours are critical." Paul survived, because they were able to stop that bleeding. Paul has now had twelve surgeries in all, the most drastic of which took place at the Mayo Clinic. They basically took out all of his organs and set them on a table. They replaced his artery from the valve in his heart all the way down to his legs and restitched every organ back into the blood supply. So he's a walking miracle.

I'll tell you, that moment when he was rushed to the ER, it was a defining moment for all of us. He was my cousin, with whom I had made all these wonderful plans. We were so excited about what the future held for us in our businesses. All of a sudden, everything changed drastically. Nothing else mattered at that moment. Nothing! All that mattered was that he recovered. Our health is such a critical piece that we often forget about it until a life-threatening event like this occurs.

He and I still have a great relationship. He's taken over his business from his dad. We've gotten rid of the old guys!

The postscript to the story is what happened with his brother, Sam, who I talked about in Chapter 4. One day he was at work and he wasn't feeling well. They rushed him to the ER and they weren't able to stop the bleeding in time, and he died of a dissected aorta, the same thing Paul had. At that moment, we realized that the condition was hereditary. They have now isolated the gene for it, so many people in our family have been tested. Paul and Sam's father, Dan, has that gene. Dan has now had elective aortic arch replacement surgery, because that's typically where an aneurism will form first. Obviously, Sam's death at thirty-eight was a huge blow to our family. Sam had been there every step of the way for Paul throughout those twelve surgeries. So I never take for granted a day or a moment with Paul or anyone I care about. That's because I saw Paul go through all those surgeries, and that was a huge struggle.

After the major surgery, Paul went into a major depression because he was feeling so much uncertainty about his health, and he had no idea when the surgeries would be over, or how many more times he would be "opened up." I remember visiting him at his home when he was recovering from that major surgery. He had all the curtains drawn and it was very dark and gloomy. I remember walking in and throwing open the curtains, because it was about time for Paul to come back to work.

I knew he was struggling. I said, "Listen, you're gonna get dressed and we're gonna go to the office, because it's time for you to get out of this house."

He shook his head. "I'm not going anywhere," he said.

"Yes, you are. Get dressed. We're going to the office. I'm going to take you in, and then I'll bring you back home, but you *are* gonna get out of this house today."

He ended up listening, and I took him to the office. He was only there for an hour and a half to two hours, and he wasn't too happy with me. Later, though, he said, "Had you not done that that day, I don't know where I would have ended up."

That's why I say your success is defined by your relationships in addition to your purpose and your health. Sometimes the people around you need to be pulled through their own defining moments because they can't see their way through them. I look back at what he went through and I wonder if I could have gone through that. I truly don't know. Twelve cardiac surgeries, and every one was extremely critical. They could have gone either way. The doctors later told us that they were basically "figuring it out" as they operated on him because very few people have gone through what he's gone through.

I'd like to share one last defining moment in this chapter. It's the moment when I became full owner of McNeely

Financial Services. This was a process I had gone through with my father. I've already discussed when he gave me some stock and allowed me to be part owner. Slowly, I moved more and more into ownership. I was at a planning retreat with my sales team in Arizona and we were working on our goals for the following year. My father lives in Arizona, and he showed up at the hotel with a bouquet of roses and a card that said, "Congratulations to the new owner of McNeely Financial Services."

I was so surprised to see him.

"What are you doing here?" I asked. He had not been part of planning retreats in years past because he had been retired.

"I had to come and give you these," he said.

Well, I cried and my whole sales team had tears in their eyes. Talk about a bursting moment! We were all so excited. That was a moment I won't forget, because I remember how difficult it was for him to let go of his company, which I've said many times he actually called his "baby." And now he was acknowledging that it was finished. It was a five-year process during which he essentially passed the torch to me, and he did it with a smile on his face because he knew we were heading in a great direction. I still keep the card that came with those flowers. I keep it on a bulletin board in the office so I can look at it when I need to remember.

So that's really it. **The point is this: *connect your dots.*** We have high moments and low moments in life. We truly ride a roller coaster. And if we plotted our life on a graph, we would see those high moments and low moments, and then we would look back and ask ourselves what we learned from them. Most people never connect their dots. They'll say, "Well, this happened, and that happened." It's a little like an investment: sometimes they go up and sometimes they correct. In our lives, we have highs and lows and corrections, too. It's important not to dwell on the past, but at the same time it's important to look at the past periodically, and in a positive way, so that you can see just how far you've come. That's why I say, connect the dots. It will make all the difference.

VALUE ADDED:
FUNDS FOR THOUGHT

While it may sound like a tall order, take some time to sit down, slow down, and reflect on your life. Write down the moments that defined it—good and bad—personal and professional—past and present. What did you learn from each one of them? Which were the bursting moments—so much so that when you think about them, you practically (or actually!) jump out of your seat. Hold onto that feeling. How can you create a life that will give you more of it?

Chapter 11

Redefining Success:
It's Always Your Choice

EARLY IN MY CAREER, MY IDEA OF SUCCESS WAS ALL
about survival. Did I have enough production coming in
to maintain everything, or at least survive? Any increased
revenue was looked upon as a gift. It's accurate to say that
in the beginning my mantra was "just help me get a sale
today to cover my bills." I might chant it under my breath
a few times a day, just for reinforcement!

I think that's how a lot of people start out. But then
as you grow into your work, the industry becomes more
about the flexibility that is one of its hallmarks, and you
can mold it into what you want it to be, so your definition
of success changes.

Sometimes that definition is a daily challenge for me: I've just got to get this done! It becomes about motivating myself to move forward versus being stuck in a rut. But more often than not my definition is broader: helping people, serving clients, helping them have greater peace of mind that can come with knowing their planning is in order. The concept of success is redefined as we understand more about what we do.

I've talked about the period of time my mom was going through cancer treatment, and at that time my measure of success—in fact the pinnacle of success—was getting to be with her. Success can evolve this way on a very personal level. The business didn't mean as much to me as it had—not that I ever lost sight of my clients' needs—but generating new business, for example, had to take a back seat to my mother's comfort and survival. During that time, my mother's idea of her own success was also redefined. She needed to marshal all of her forces to fight the disease, recuperate—including regaining her strength following chemo and radiation—and return to the work she'd come to love over a thirty-year career in insurance and financial services.

In Chapter 10, I talked about my cousin Paul's brush with death, resulting disability, and about a dozen lifesaving surgeries that all but consumed him—and me. We'd been extremely close since childhood and were in the industry together, making plans that would keep us working side by side. During the extended period of time he was ill, while work had to go on, again my definition of success changed as I focused on helping him get through his ordeal (even when he didn't want me around!) at all costs.

In short, the act of redefining success is challenging, ongoing, evolving—or at least it should be. Success is about touching lives, making a difference, and appreciating what we have.

§

To stay motivated, it's important to keep looking forward, setting goals, and asking ourselves what's next in order to redefine success. For some, this is not their idea of fun because they prefer their comfort level, the familiar, and maintaining the status quo. For me, what's next has always been the driver. The question of what I can do to keep the momentum going occurs to me over and over, and I act on it.

Though it was a long process, taking over the business from my father was a very big "what's next" for me. I left a solid (though unfulfilling) position in banking, where I'd found a measure of success, to return home to learn how to be successful in financial services. Through several indescribably daunting years I had to keep renewing my commitment to becoming worthy of owning and running a financial services business—one that my father had built and run for many years. At age twenty-eight, and though I'd been a professional

129

for five years, I was an absolute beginner when I stepped through that door on my first day. As time wore on and I became increasingly discouraged, I would sometimes think about Steve Jobs, who had dropped out of college and, at age thirty, had been fired from the company he founded.

"I didn't see it then, but it turned out that getting fired was the best thing that could ever have happened to me," he once said. "The heaviness of being successful was replaced by the lightness of being a beginner again, less sure about everything. It freed me to enter one of the most creative periods of my life."[1]

While I hadn't been fired, I, too, was a beginner, and though I wasn't fully aware of it at first, I was free to create my life exactly as I wanted it to be.

This book is a shining example of what was next for me—how I could keep redefining my success. In the process of deciding to write it—which is a manifestation of my reaching for the next rung on my career ladder—I spent months and years consciously (and maybe subconsciously) gearing up: collecting information, making sure I had the kind of experiences readers would want to know about and from which they could benefit, writing down observations and reflections on what had happened to me, around me in a related sense, and what I'd done with it all. If I wrote

---

[1] http://www.movemequotes.com/top-10-steve-jobs-quotes/

a book, my goal was to have it be as inspirational as it was aspirational—to motivate and empower every woman and in fact everyone who read it. I wanted my reaching higher and further to serve as the springboard for the reader to reach higher and further.

If you ask various people in your life about success, chances are their responses will be quite different. Your boss will tell you it's about meeting production goals, seeing clients, fact-finding, and/or meeting whatever quotas make money for the company. That's the work filter.

Your spouse and children may gauge success by that family vacation for which you scrimped and saved, or even if you didn't have to do that, if you were able to set aside the time to actually take it. For most families success is defined by the time allocated to spend together—maybe carving out some hours to attend school productions or sports activities with your children versus not being able to do that. Balance is important, and if all you focus on is work, something else is probably going to fail, such as your family relationships. In life we have many masters: work, spouse, children, maybe aging parents, continuing education, community commitments—everyone and everything requiring time. And that's the gift of a career in financial services: if you are organized, focused, and disciplined, based on the industry's flexibility factor you can achieve success in everything you do.

It's important to note that the biggest mistake in defining (and redefining) success is if we allow others—who are filtering success through their own lenses—to set our definition of it. When I first began exploring the idea of success in my "Success on PURPOSE" talks, I would ask groups of people what their definitions were. I'd also ask if they thought I was successful. It was an eye-opening exercise to find out what people thought success meant.

There were times in my life when I definitely did not feel I was a success. I didn't make enough money; I hadn't made as much as another advisor; I hadn't gotten the designation another advisor had. I used to tell myself, okay, if I do all that I'll be successful. **But the definition of success is an internal one: no one can establish it for you but you.** You can have others help and guide you, and perhaps even set goals about what it looks like, but you've got to be the moment-by-moment driver. As long as you have an occupation that can support your lifestyle, and really be purpose-filled so that you can find fulfillment in it, you can master all the areas of your life.

Another component of redefining success is *choice*. One of my first jobs out of college was working as a word processor because it was the only job I could find. It was soul stifling! We can't have a world of nothing but entrepreneurs, but I knew at that time it was not going to be a job that I would do for the rest of my life. I didn't want to live with that empty feeling. When I worked at the bank, again my role was defined, my hours were defined, my job description was defined—there were so many things about that job that felt confining. To some extent I found success there, but I didn't feel as if I did because someone else had defined all that for me and presumably everyone else who would occupy that position. But with my job in financial services, the sky's the limit, and that's the message for someone brand-new to or even just considering this industry. **This career allows you to determine the parameters of your success—at all times and in all things.**

In Chapter 1 I talked about how I'd believed in my own failure rather than my success. At the outset of my career, I'm not sure I had a real idea of what success was and how to measure it. I had no concept about how to have it expand and evolve so that my life was as rich in every respect as it could possibly be. It was dedication and experience that helped me define my success and broaden my perspective, and it was the financial services industry that gave me the opportunity to measure and redefine success any way I chose, and continue to choose.

So right now, how do you define success? What does success look like for you? If you were brutally honest with yourself, is this your definition of success or has someone else put it there?

In 2013, the average age for financial services industry recruits was forty-four.[2] Clearly this is an industry that welcomes you in mid-career. Though the economy is slowly recovering and there are fewer layoffs and less downsizing, how we work has changed drastically. People in their forties, some of whom have been shifted out of a position they may have held for a long time, are looking for something new—something over which they have more control this time. One advantage for someone in that age group is that the life and professional experience they've had brings a lot to the table, right out of the starting gate. While there are no shortcuts to real success, and most advisors agree it takes at least two years to find your sea legs in the industry and at least three for the job to really start working for you, success in those first years can be defined as the patience, determination, and dedication to make it happen.

Unfortunately, as it takes time to build a career and the kind of income that's wholly possible in financial services, there is a high turnover, with women leading their male counterparts in that respect. Earlier in the book I talked about negative voices, which are a particular problem for women. While it is speculation on my part that this is a contributing factor in a higher female exodus, the bottom

---

[2] Susan M. Cooper. What Women Need To Be Successful in the Financial Services Industry with a Special Focus on Millennial Women. November 2, 2015.

line is it takes a lot of internal drive to push through those first few years. I'm the first to admit I almost didn't make it. Training, as I addressed in Chapter 2, is not geared toward the qualities women tend to bring to the profession. Maybe another measure of success lies in knowing that going in and figuring out how to adapt the training to your needs anyway.

The members of my study group have been redefining success at least as long as we've been together. Our efforts and achievements on the professional and personal fronts, and our choice to frame them as lessons and springboards, make redefining success a necessary, frequent occurrence. In Chapter 10 I talked about the five Rs. One of them is respect. In redefining your success, it is important to respect whatever lessons you learn for what they are. A lesson may be exciting or it may be a profoundly negative experience. If it is the latter, chances are you'll know how to structure things differently the next time.

Whatever success looks like for you, waking up each day with the freedom and flexibility to modify or expand it to fit whatever is going on is itself a form of success. You are in charge of your life. There aren't a lot of professions where that is possible, but with a career in financial services, you have that option.

Perhaps choosing and then reading this book to the end can be perceived as defining moments for you, as explained in the previous chapter. If my experience has resonated—maybe lit a small fire, opened you to the wealth of possibilities ahead, and launched you in a better direction for your life— consider yourself successful already. There is an industry poised and ready to ensure a lot more of it. And remember that in the financial services industry, there is **No Necktie Needed.** Welcome!

CPSIA information can be obtained
at www.ICGtesting.com
Printed in the USA
FFOW05n2331150516

9 780692 681824